PREVENTING STUDENTS FROM DROPPING OUT

Alexander W. Astin

PREVENTING STUDENTS FROM DROPPING OUT

Jossey-Bass Publishers
San Francisco • Washington • London • 1975

The
Jossey-Bass Series
in Higher Education

PREFACE

Dropping out of college has been a much-researched topic, but the research has not clearly revealed which factors influence students to leave or how these factors might be controlled by those with a vested interest in preventing students from leaving. Thus, the research reported here focuses primarily on identifying ways to help students finish college. The principal findings are addressed to three categories of decision-makers who have an interest in the dropout problem and who are in a position to choose particular courses of action to improve students' chances of completing college: institutional administrators, educational planners and policy-makers at state and national levels, and students and guidance counselors.

In the first category are those staff members of colleges and universities who make decisions affecting students' chances of finishing: presidents, vice-presidents, deans, registrars, admissions officers, directors of financial aid, and student personnel officers. Since faculty groups also make some of these decisions, many faculty members are among this policy-making group. And members of boards of trustees often ratify if they do not initiate these decisions.

The data reported here indicate that the students' chances of finishing can be influenced by a wide range of institutional practices: recruitment and admissions policies, residence requirements, allocation of financial aid, selection of students for residence halls, availability of jobs on campus, grading practices, granting of leaves of absence, transfer policies, and establishment of work-study programs.

Educational policy-makers are persons whose decisions affect a number of institutions simultaneously: legislators, administrators in the executive branches, and advisors to these legislators and administrators. They may operate at the national, state, or local level. Although their decisions are frequently directed at the public institutions over which they have jurisdiction, most of their actions also have important implications for privately controlled institutions.

These policy-makers often have to choose among alternatives that can substantially influence national and institutional dropout rates: alternatives regarding student financial aid, admissions, construction of residential facilities, tuition levels, and development of new institutions. The number of dropouts that can be salvaged by a given amount of financial aid, for example, depends on how that aid is distributed among various programs (grants versus loans versus work-study) and on how student eligibility is determined. The research findings show not only which policies are most likely to minimize the number of student dropouts, but also what the magnitudes are in numbers and percentages of dropouts salvaged.

One problem confronting policy-makers at the state and local levels is how to evaluate the relative dropout rates of the different institutions for which they are responsible. Are those institutions with relatively high dropout rates doing a poor job, or are their rates simply a result of the types of students who attend? This study provides policy-makers with an objective means to assess dropout rates based on the characteristics of the students who are admitted.

Although students clearly have an interest in improving their chances of completing college, they are seldom, if ever, in a position to influence those national policies and institutional practices that could help them. Nevertheless, students do make certain critical decisions. Perhaps the most important choice is the type of college to attend. Deciding on a two-year rather than a four-year college or university, a public rather than a private institution, or a large rather than a small college has important consequences.

Whether to commute to college or to live away from home is another decision that can substantially affect chances of graduating.

Rather than being aimed at an amorphous category that includes all student decision-makers, the findings of this study are presented separately for different types of students. The study shows, for example, that men who choose certain options can expect a result somewhat different from the outcome for women who select the same options. Similarly, certain choices tend to affect black and white students differently. Thus, this study gives students—black and nonblack, men and women—a practical means of estimating their own chances of dropping out. Where appropriate, it presents results separately for students of varying ability and income levels.

A fourth audience toward which this study is directed is the community of social scientists and educational researchers. The research reported here includes features not combined in any previous single study of dropouts: a representative national sample of students and institutions; multivariate controls over student input characteristics and over environmental contingencies such as financial aid, work, and residence during college; and a definition of the term *dropout* which avoids some of the pitfalls of traditional definitions. Although these refinements do, I believe, contribute significantly to understanding the dropout phenomenon, there is still a long way to go. Thus, the final chapter contains suggestions for future research which should provide further clues for decision making by administrators, policy-makers, and prospective students and their guidance counselors.

While it has become fashionable to talk of stopping out and of the supposedly therapeutic value for certain students of dropping out, this book basically skirts the argument over the "good" versus the "bad" dropout; the reader does not have to take a position on this issue to utilize the findings. I assume that many decision-makers—faculty members and administrators, educational policy-makers, prospective college students, and guidance counselors—want to increase the probability that entrants will graduate. To do so, they must select those actions associated with persistence and avoid those associated with dropping out.

Preventing Students from Dropping Out is organized as follows: Chapter One discusses the design of the study, presents detailed definitions of three basic terms (dropout, stopout, and persister), analyzes students' reasons for dropping out, and summarizes the current employment and marital status of dropouts. Chapter Two gives the results of a multivariate analysis of some one hundred student characteristics reported at the time of college entry. These measures are combined to form an estimate of "dropout-proneness," which acts as a control in analyses of the influence of alternative decisions in subsequent chapters. Chapter Three examines the impact on persistence of various forms of financial aid, and Chapter Four portrays the impact of employment. Chapter Five treats the effects of residence, academic achievement, and participation in extracurricular activities.

In Chapter Six persistence is related to type of college; Chapter Seven extends this analysis to the overall "fit" between student and college. The final chapter (Chapter Eight) summarizes implications for each category of decision-maker (institutional administrators and faculty members, educational policy-makers, and prospective college students) and concludes with suggestions for future research on the dropout phenomenon.

This study is an outgrowth of a long-term series of national studies of college students which began in the early 1960s at the National Merit Scholarship Corporation and moved to the American Council on Education (ACE) in 1965. The Cooperative Institutional Research Program (CIRP) is now one of the largest ongoing longitudinal studies in education (currently involving nearly three million students and more than nine hundred institutions). My former ACE colleagues Robert J. Panos and John A. Creager were instrumental in getting this program off the ground, and the strong support of Logan Wilson and Allan Cartter during the early years was critical. (Data in the current study are from a longitudinal cohort made up of 1968 freshmen who were followed up in 1972.)

The movement of CIRP from ACE to the Laboratory for Research on Higher Education at the University of California, Los Angeles, in the summer of 1973 would not have been possible without the continued support and backing of ACE President Roger

Heyns and the board of directors. This book is one of the first major projects carried out at UCLA.

Among the persons whose help contributed substantially to the production of this work are Margo R. King, who accommodated the chaotic lifestyle of the author in her usual highly competent fashion; Gerald T. Richardson, John M. Light, and Paul Hemond, who carried out the extraordinarily complicated data analyses; Carol E. Christian, who helped with bibliographical material and data analysis; JB Lon Hefferlin, who gave several valuable suggestions concerning content and organization of the text; and Beverly T. Watkins, whose editing of some rough drafts made them eminently more readable.

Finally, an expression of thanks for a number of valuable suggestions and conversations is due to Lena Astin, who never disrupts our home life as much with her books as I do with mine.

Los Angeles   ALEXANDER W. ASTIN
March 1975

CONTENTS

PREVENTING STUDENTS FROM DROPPING OUT

1

THE WHO AND WHY
OF DROPPING OUT

Dropping out of college is a little like the weather: something everyone talks about but no one does anything about. This predilection for talk over action is reflected in much of the research on dropouts, which has focused more on counting, describing, and classifying them than on seeking solutions to the problem. The national study of dropouts which provides the principal factual basis for this book takes a somewhat different approach. Rather than simply tabulating rates or describing student characteristics, it seeks to identify practical measures to minimize students' chances of dropping out.

As critics have rightly pointed out, for some students leaving college before completing a degree may be highly beneficial to personal development. While such an interpretation is valid in certain cases, this study takes the position that many decision-makers—students included—legitimately want to know more about how to increase students' chances of finishing college, whether this concern is based on the loss of talent, the waste of limited educational resources, or the vocational and personal setbacks that result from the student's impeded career development and futile expenditure of time and effort.

1

Another factor that prompts attention to the dropout problem—perhaps the biggest concern of college administrators and faculty members during the 1970s—is declining enrollment. In most private institutions, income derives largely from tuition and fees; therefore, each new student brings additional income, and each student retained maintains this income. In the public sector, the bulk of income derives from state appropriations, which are usually allocated in direct proportion to projected enrollments.

Adjusting to enrollments that are tapering off is particularly difficult because many public and private institutions became accustomed in the 1960s to rapid expansion. While a 10 percent increase in enrollment may bring close to a 10 percent increase in revenue, the associated increase in costs will generally be far less. Thus, the net effect of increasing enrollments is to generate what amounts to discretionary funds. The problem here is that this process does not work in reverse. A 10 percent decline in enrollment, which is generally accompanied by close to a 10 percent decline in revenue, is *not* accompanied by a 10 percent reduction in costs. Under these conditions, adapting to a pattern of steady or even declining enrollments after being used to yearly increases has been traumatic for many institutions.

While administrators and faculty have traditionally seen recruitment as the principal means to keeping enrollments up, an equally promising approach is to reduce dropout rates. Note that, in four-year institutions, any change that deters students from dropping out can affect three classes of students at once, whereas any change in recruiting practices can affect only one class in a given year. From this viewpoint, investing resources to prevent dropping out may be more "cost effective" than applying the same resources to more vigorous recruitment. More important from an educational standpoint, changes that help students complete college represent a real service to them, whereas successful recruiting efforts may simply change students' choice of institution.

Design of the Study

The sheer volume of research on college dropouts might tempt one to conclude that much is known about factors that influence students to leave college before completing their degrees.

But most published research is limited in scope and inadequate in design. The principal deficiency is the lack of a longitudinal design and the use of only one or a limited number of institutions. Longitudinal data (those resulting from repeated assessment of the same students at several points in time) permit one to track the student from the time of matriculation through the expected time of degree completion. Such data make it possible to compare the environmental experiences of dropouts and persisters and to control for initial differences among students when they first enter college. By including a variety of institutions, the investigator can examine the possible impact of institutional characteristics, such as type (two-year versus four-year, for example), size, and so forth.

The data in this particular study are both longitudinal and multiinstitutional. Research subjects, selected from 1968 entering freshmen, were surveyed initially in fall 1968 and followed up four years later in summer and fall 1972. These students were selected from a representative national sample of 358 two- and four-year colleges and universities. (For a complete description of the sampling design and other technical details, see Astin, 1975.) These institutions were participants in the Cooperative Institutional Research Program, conducted jointly by the Laboratory for Research on Higher Education at the University of California, Los Angeles, and the American Council on Education.

The original freshman sample included 243,156 students. Because of budgetary limitations, it was not possible to follow up the entire sample. Therefore, samples of approximately 300 students were selected randomly from each institution for a follow-up of approximately 101,000 students in 1972. (All students were followed up in those institutions with freshman class enrollments below 300, and, to have longitudinal data on a substantial number of blacks, all 16,544 black students were included in the follow-up sample.)

Questionnaires were mailed in late summer and fall 1972 from the American Council on Education to each student's home address as provided on the original questionnaire completed four years earlier. First-class postage was used so mail would be forwarded to students who had moved. A reminder postcard was sent to each student approximately one week after the initial questionnaire was mailed, and a second questionnaire was sent to nonrespondents about one month later.

In addition to data from the freshman and follow-up questionnaires, each institution provided students' scores on the Scholastic Aptitude Test (SAT) and American College Test (ACT), as well as information on whether or not they had completed the baccalaureate degree at the time of the 1972 follow-up.

Of the questionnaires returned, 41,356 were properly completed and used in the longitudinal study. To adjust for any bias that might be introduced by differences between respondents and nonrespondents, complex weighting procedures were applied to the data from the 41,356 respondents.[1] Independent studies (Astin and Molm, 1972) indicate that these procedures correct much of the bias that results from nonresponse to mailed surveys. The method depends, of course, on having a large amount of prior information on both respondents and nonrespondents. Since the data provided by the institutions on each student's degree status as of 1972 were also included in the weighting procedures, the weighted data are probably reasonably accurate indicators of the actual dropout and persistence rates in the total college population.

The questionnaire completed by the students when they entered college as freshmen in fall 1968 included approximately 175 items covering such background information as age, sex, race, religion, and past achievements, as well as parents' income, education, and occupation. The form also asked questions about the student's educational and career plans, study habits, life goals, daily activities, reasons for choosing the college, sources of financial aid,

---

[1] The basic purpose of these procedures is to develop a set of weights which will give the greatest weight to the data of those respondents who most resemble nonrespondents in terms of their freshman data. Thus, since minority students from relatively poor socioeconomic backgrounds and with relatively low high school grade averages were least likely to respond, the data from such students were given the largest weights, whereas more affluent nonminority students with relatively good grades were given the smallest weights. These weights were further adjusted to reflect the undersampling of nonblack students in the follow-up and to compensate for the differential sampling of students in the larger institutions and the differential sampling of institutions in the original stratification design. For a detailed description of these procedures, see Astin and Molm (1972).

and self-predictions about possible college outcomes (including estimates of the chances of dropping out temporarily or permanently).

The follow-up questionnaire contained questions about the students' educational progress since entering college: number of years of undergraduate attendance, degrees earned, current degree plans, and a year-by-year record of enrollment status. It also contained items on how students had financed their undergraduate education, where they had lived each year since entering college, and types of jobs held. (The freshman questionnaire and the follow-up questionnaire are available from the author at the Graduate School of Education, University of California, Los Angeles.)

Analyses of these longitudinal data involved several steps. The first was to utilize each entering student's personal background data (1968 questionnaire data plus SAT and ACT scores) to develop quantitative estimates of the student's chances of dropping out of college (see Chapter Two for these results). The final steps were attempts to identify alternative environmental experiences that further influenced the student's chances of dropping out, that is, experiences that increased or decreased the estimates of dropout probabilities based on the student's personal characteristics. These results are treated in separate chapters on different types of environmental experiences: the impact of alternative types of financial aid, work experience, residence and the campus environment, institutional characteristics, and the "fit" between the student and the institutional environment. The final chapter summarizes the major findings in terms of their implications for students, institutional administrators, and policy-makers.

Who Is a Dropout?

A key aspect of any dropout study is defining its central subject. This chapter provides a detailed exposition of the particular definition used in this study, and—in order to provide a broader context within which to view the definition—concludes with an analysis of reasons given by the dropouts for leaving college and a summary of their current status.

The major definitional problem is the temporariness of any

classification of a student as a dropout. No categorization will be wholly satisfactory until all students either obtain their degrees or die without receiving them: any former student can, in theory, go back to college at any time to complete the degree. This study copes with this obstacle by identifying three rather than two classes of students: those who are clearly not dropouts, those who are clearly dropouts, and an ambiguous group that has interrupted its undergraduate education but has a reasonable chance of completing degrees in the near future—a group labeled *stopouts.*

Another difficulty involves students' own goals and plans. For example, traditional studies of college dropouts have failed to consider differences in students' initial educational aspirations. Some students, of course, enter college with no intention of obtaining a degree. When these students leave without a degree, it seems inappropriate to label them dropouts, particularly in view of the pejorative connotation the term acquires when it is used to suggest that the students have been unable to fulfill their initial expectations. Thus, this study considers as dropouts only those students who had originally planned to earn a bachelor's degree but who subsequently failed to do so.

To elucidate how this study arrived at its definitions, let us look at the relationship between initial expectations and subsequent attainments. Table 1 shows that four years after entering college in fall 1968, almost half (49.6 percent) the sample students are either enrolled in graduate or professional school or have their bachelor's degrees. (A few students admitted to graduate or professional school without bachelor's degrees are included.) The students' initial degree plans are strongly associated with their chances of getting a degree within four years. Thus, among freshmen who aspire to no degree beyond an associate degree, only one in eight is enrolled in graduate school or had a bachelor's degree four years later, compared to more than six in eight among students who initially aspire to a doctorate or advanced professional degree.[2] (In these and all

---

[2] It is surprising that students' chances of obtaining a bachelor's degree are substantially greater among those who say they are planning *no* degree (three in eight) than among those who initially aspire to an associate degree (one in eight). Apparently, this "no degree" group includes a number of students whose educational plans are not crystalized at matriculation and

Table 1.

DEGREE-COMPLETION RATES AS A FUNCTION OF DEGREE PLANS
(Weighted Population Estimates for 1968 Entering Freshmen)'

Highest Degree Planned Fall 1968	N (Percentage of Total Population)	Percentage Holding Bachelor's Degrees and/or Enrolled in Graduate or Professional School in Fall 1972
None	66,500 (5.0)	35.6
Associate	85,308 (6.4)	12.5
Bachelor's*	538,656 (40.4)	45.4
Master's	417,260 (31.3)	58.3
Doctoral or advanced professional	226,094 (17.0)	61.8
Total	1,333,818(100.0)	49.6

* Includes students who checked "other" degree.

subsequent analyses, only the weighted population estimates are provided. For a detailed discussion of the effects of these weighting procedures on the dropout figures, see Astin, 1975.)

The low rates of baccalaureate degree completion among the two groups that initially aspire to less than a bachelor's degree support the assumption that in certain respects their members are not comparable to entering college students who do aspire to a bachelor's (or higher) degree. Consequently, these groups have been excluded from subsequent analyses.[3] Thus, the remaining group

who subsequently decide to pursue the bachelor's or some higher degree. Students who initially aspire to the associate degree are apparently much more likely to stick to their initial plans and not to raise their aspirations once they start college. (Most of this latter group enroll initially in two-year or community colleges.)

[3] Analyses of the "dropin" phenomenon—the factors that influence students who initially did not plan a bachelor's degree to change their minds —are under way at the Laboratory for Research on Higher Education at the

consists of students who initially aspired to at least a bachelor's degree. The term *dropout* is more appropriately applied to students within this limited group.

Eliminating the 11.4 percent of the students who did not initially aspire to at least a bachelor's degree has little effect on the sex or racial composition of the entering student population. The percentage of men shifts slightly upward (from 57.3 percent to 57.6 percent), which reflects the fact that men are somewhat more likely than women to plan initially on at least a bachelor's degree when they enter college. The racial composition of the sample changes even less: the concentration of white students remains about the same (90 percent), the concentration of blacks shifts slightly upward (from 7 percent to 7.2 percent), and the percentage of "other" minorities shifts slightly downward (from 3 percent to 2.8 percent). These changes indicate that blacks are a little more likely than whites and other minorities to seek at least the bachelor's degree at the time they first enter college. Similar findings have been reported by several investigators (Bayer and Boruch, 1969).

For this study the available follow-up data are detailed enough to permit development of relatively unambiguous measures of student persistence. In addition to information about the student's degree completion and enrollment in graduate or professional school, the follow-up questionnaire includes queries about years of college completed since 1968, whether or not the student has been enrolled continuously since 1968, whether the student is currently enrolled full time as an undergraduate, and what degree the student is seeking.

Readers should keep in mind that students were asked two different questions about their past undergraduate enrollment. In one the students indicated whether they had been enrolled full time or part time or both during each of the four academic years; those who had attended at least part time each year were classified as being "continuously enrolled since 1968." In the other question, students were asked simply to indicate how many years of college they had completed since 1968. These two figures could be different

University of California, Los Angeles. For this study of dropouts, however, such students were excluded to make possible a more useful definition of dropout.

if the student had an accelerated undergraduate program, took a reduced course load, or failed a number of courses.

Three categories of educational attainment were developed from the students' responses.

A *persister* is defined as any student who, at the time of the 1972 follow-up, satisfies one of the following conditions: (1) is enrolled full time in graduate or professional school; (2) has earned the B.A. (or a higher) degree; or (3) has completed four years of college, is still enrolled full time, and is still pursuing at least the bachelor's degree.

For the second category, the currently popular neologism *stopout* has been chosen. This term presents some definitional problems, since its meaning is somewhat ambiguous. Stopouts include students who interrupt their undergraduate education for a relatively brief period and return to complete the degree. Some institutions have developed programs that encourage certain students to stop out. Although the wisdom of advising students to interrupt their college education is a matter of some debate, one major objective of stopout programs is to facilitate reenrollment. Stopouts who return and complete their degrees become persisters; those who subsequently fail to return or who abandon their plans for the degree become dropouts. Thus, stopping out is a temporary status.

A *stopout* is defined as any nonpersister who is still planning to obtain at least a bachelor's degree at the time of the 1972 follow-up *and* who satisfies one of the following conditions: (1) is enrolled full time as an undergraduate; (2) has completed four years of undergraduate work since 1968; or (3) has been continuously enrolled (full or part time) since 1968.

About the rationale for defining a stopout by these criteria: since stopouts are those who leave college temporarily, the definition should cover those currently enrolled in fall 1972 but not continuously enrolled since entering college in 1968. At the same time, the definition should also include persons not currently enrolled but continuously enrolled from fall 1968 to fall 1972 who still intend to obtain the degree. These persons probably have a good chance of returning and completing any additional work needed for the degree.

One percent of the total sample—those students who are still enrolled at the time of the 1972 follow-up but who report that they no longer intend to get a bachelor's (or higher) degree—presents a classification problem. Classifying this small group as dropouts seems questionable, given the fact that these students were enrolled as full-time undergraduates at the time of the follow-up. Consequently, they have been included with the stopouts. The finding that 44 percent of this small group had actually completed four undergraduate years since 1968 and that 78 percent had completed three or more years of college reinforces this decision.

The third category of educational attainment, the *dropouts*, includes all students who cannot be classified as either persisters or stopouts. Thus, a dropout is any student who: (1) is not enrolled in graduate or professional school; (2) does not have a bachelor's (or higher) degree; (3) is not currently enrolled full time as an undergraduate; *and* (4) has not been continuously enrolled since 1968; (5) has not completed four years of undergraduate work since 1968; and/or (6) is no longer pursuing the bachelor's (or a higher) degree.

A nonpersister can avoid classification as a dropout by continuous enrollment (full or part time) for four years, by current full-time enrollment, or by completion of four years of undergraduate work.

Readers should keep in mind that the "dropouts" in this study include both students who leave college voluntarily and those who are forced to leave because of poor grades or for disciplinary reasons. In many instances it is difficult to distinguish between the two groups since some students may "voluntarily" leave in anticipation of receiving grades that would force them to withdraw, whereas others may let their grades drop to the failure level because they have already decided to leave college for other (nonacademic) reasons.

Table 2 shows the national percentages of persisters, stopouts, and dropouts after four years. About two students in three (65.0 percent) are persisters; one in ten (10.9 percent) is a stopout; and the rest—one student in four (24.3 percent)—become dropouts. These figures suggest that the ability of students to persist in college has not, as some observers have claimed, deteriorated in recent

Table 2.
Educational Attainment Four Years After Entering College (1968 Entering Freshmen)
(Percentages)

Status* Fall 1972	Men (N = 681,281**)	Women (N = 500,611**)	All Students (N = 1,181,892**)
PERSISTERS			
Are enrolled in graduate or professional school	13.1	10.3	11.9
Have completed bachelor's degree, are not in graduate school	34.9	49.6	41.2
Have completed four years, are enrolled full time and desire bachelor's (or higher) degree	14.4	8.4	11.9
STOPOUTS			
Have completed *fewer* than four years, are enrolled full time and desire bachelor's (or higher) degree	4.2	3.7	4.0
Have completed four years, are *not* enrolled full time and desire bachelor's (or higher) degree	4.3	2.6	3.6
Were enrolled full time for four years, are *not now* enrolled and desire bachelor's (or higher) degree	1.2	.8	1.1
Were enrolled full *or* part time for four years, are *not now* enrolled and desire bachelor's (or higher) degree	1.4	1.0	1.2
Currently enrolled full time, *not* pursuing bachelor's (or higher) degree	1.1	.8	1.0
DROPOUTS			
Not currently enrolled, pursuing bachelor's (or higher) degree	11.3	9.3	10.5
Not currently enrolled, *not* pursuing bachelor's (or higher) degree	14.1	13.5	13.8

* Each "status" is mutually exclusive, that is, students with any given status fail to satisfy the criteria for statuses higher on the list.
** Ns and percentages are weighted population estimates for all 1968 full-time entering freshmen who aspired to at least the bachelor's degree at time of matriculation.

years. More than half the students actually finish their undergraduate work within four years after entering college, and another
12 percent—those who have completed four years of college and are
still enrolled in full-time study toward a degree—are likely to finish
their degrees within another year or so. Of the one-quarter classified
as dropouts, nearly half say they plan eventually to return to college
to get a degree. Although the figures are not precisely comparable,
data from earlier studies (Astin, 1972a; Astin and Panos, 1969;
and Bayer, Royer, and Webb, 1973) indicate that persistence
among college students has, if anything, increased during recent
years.

Thus, even if students who initially aspired to the associate
degree or to no degree are included, the percentage of students
entering four-year colleges and universities who obtain a bachelor's
degree in four years is slightly higher among freshmen of 1968 than
among freshmen of 1961 (Astin and Panos, 1969). Whether this
finding is the result of some temporary phenomenon (the draft, for
example) or indicative of a more lasting trend can be determined
only in future longitudinal studies.

Table 2 reveals some notable sex differences in educational
attainment. Women are much more likely than men to complete the
bachelor's degree in four years. Even if those men who do not have
a degree but who have been enrolled continuously since 1968 and
are currently pursuing degrees (many were probably in five-year
programs, such as engineering or architecture) are included among
the persisters, women show a persistence rate about 5 percent higher
than that for men (68.3 percent versus 62.4 percent). Under these
circumstances, it is surprising that the graduate school attendance
rate is about 3 percent higher among men than among women.
Clearly, the relative loss of women in the transition from undergraduate to graduate study is substantial.

Table 3 shows the years of college completed since 1968 for
persisters, stopouts, and dropouts. These data are consistent with
the three definitions: of all three groups of persisters (the first three
columns), more than 80 percent report completing four or more
years of college, and more than 98 percent report completing three
or more years. These figures contrast sharply with the result for

Table 3.

CUMULATIVE YEARS OF COLLEGE COMPLETED BY STUDENTS
AT VARIOUS LEVELS OF EDUCATIONAL ATTAINMENT
(Percentages)

| | Level of Educational Attainment Fall 1972 | | | | |
| | Persisters | | | | |
Years of College Completed Since 1968	Enrolled in Graduate or Professional School	Completed Bachelor's Degree (Not in Graduate School)	Never Left College Since 1968; Currently Pursuing B.A. or B.S. Full Time	Stopouts	Dropouts
One or more	100.0	99.9	100.0	98.3	89.1
1½ or more	99.4	99.8	100.0	96.9	72.7
2 or more	99.4	99.8	99.8	92.6	58.4
2½ or more	98.6	99.7	99.5	85.8	35.1
3 or more	98.2	99.4	98.5	77.4	21.5
3½ or more	93.5	94.8	94.1	56.7	8.4
4 or more	88.3	87.5	82.7	37.3	3.0

stopouts: only 37.3 percent report completing four or more years of college. Also, since more than three-fourths of the stopouts report completing at least three years of college, one would expect many of these persons eventually to become persisters. Dropouts, of course, complete the fewest years of college: only 3 percent report completing four or more years, and only about one in five reports completing three or more years.

The finding that more than 10 percent of the students who either have obtained bachelor's degrees or are enrolled in graduate or professional school have completed fewer than four years of college is somewhat unexpected. Their receipt of the baccalaureate is no doubt attributable in part to accelerated undergraduate programs such as those recommended recently by the Carnegie Commission on Higher Education (1972). Their enrollment in further education occurs in those graduate and professional schools that admit students who do not have baccalaureate degrees or who have completed fewer than four years of undergraduate work.

Students' Reasons for Dropping Out

Dropout studies that are not longitudinal in design typically emphasize the explanations provided by students for dropping out. To accept such post hoc interpretations at face value is a questionable practice, considering the complexity of the dropout phenomenon and the natural tendency for persons to rationalize behavior which might be regarded by others as evidence of failure. Data of this type are useful, however, in suggesting some of the antecedent precipitating factors that may prompt students to leave college.

In the follow-up questionnaire, students were asked to check not more than three of twelve reasons for dropping out of college. The twelve reasons, with the percentages of men and women dropouts who checked each, are:

	Men	Women	All Students
Boredom with courses	36	25	32
Financial difficulties	29	27	28
Some other reason	31	24	28
Marriage, pregnancy, or other family responsibilities	11	39	23
Poor grades	28	14	22
Dissatisfaction with requirements or regulations	24	20	22
Change in career goals	19	20	19
Inability to take desired courses or programs	12	9	11
Good job offer	10	6	9
Illness or accident	7	7	7
Difficulty commuting to college	3	3	3
Disciplinary troubles	2	2	2

The most frequent reasons for dropping out for both men and women are boredom with courses, financial difficulties, dissatisfaction with requirements or regulations, and change in career goals. Women, however, give marriage, pregnancy, or other family responsibilities more often than any other reason (this item was eighth in importance for men). Poor grades is fourth in importance for men, but seventh in importance for women (only half as many women as men check this reason). The fact that "some other reason" was checked relatively often suggests that one or more important reasons (for example, personal or emotional problems) were missing from the list. Although the methodology and sampling differ from those in earlier studies, these results on the relative importance of various factors in dropping out are generally consistent with results from several older studies summarized by Summerskill (1962). The major discrepancy is in the importance attributed to academic difficulties: only 22 percent of students in the current study, in contrast with a median of about 33 percent in the studies reviewed by Summerskill, cited poor academic performance as a reason for dropping out.

The finding that women are three times more likely than men to give marriage as a reason for dropping out of college supports a number of earlier studies (for example, see Bayer, 1969). Getting married while in college is one of the most important determinants of dropping out for women, but of little or no importance for men (see Chapter Four).

One might argue, of course, that women give marriage as a reason for dropping out more often than do men because more women actually get married. That this explanation is not valid is revealed by the following data: among dropouts who report that they are married, the percentage of women who say they left college because of marriage (59) is still much higher than the percentage of men who give this reason (26).

A related question is the role of children. Does the number of children have any effect on the dropout's tendency to give marriage, pregnancy, or other family responsibilities as a reason for leaving college? To examine this question, married dropouts were sorted by number of children at the time of the follow-up, and the

proportion that gave marriage as a reason for leaving college was
determined for each group.

	Men	*Women*
No children	16	45
One child	37	71
Two children	39	68
Three or more children	39	69

These data show clearly that having children increases the
dropout's chances of giving marriage as a reason for leaving college.
The effect occurs among both sexes, although women are consistently more likely to give this particular reason. The *number* of
children (that is, one, two, three or more) bears little or no relationship to the students' chances of giving marriage as a reason for
leaving college. The principal difference is between students with no
children and students with one or more. Even though having children greatly increases the married students' tendency to give marriage as a reason for leaving college, fully 45 percent of the married
women with no children (compared with only 16 percent of the
married men with no children) give marriage as a reason for
leaving.

The finding that men are much more likely than women to
give poor grades as a reason for dropping out is consistent with
numerous earlier studies showing that women get better grades than
men both in high school and in college. The student's undergraduate gradepoint average, in turn, bears a close relationship to
dropping out (see Chapter Five).

That financial difficulties are checked by more than one-
fourth of the dropouts of both sexes suggests that improved
financial aid programs may offer one possible solution to the dropout problem, at least for some students. Certain types of financial
aid appear to facilitate student peristence in college, while other
forms seem to have a negative effect (see Chapter Three).

Although both men and women tend to give boredom with
courses or dissatisfaction with requirements or regulations relatively

often as reasons for leaving college, men are somewhat more inclined than women toward such reasons. One can argue that boredom or dissatisfaction with requirements represents a handy rationalization for failure which in reality is attributable to other causes (poor academic performance, for example). There is, in fact, a slight tendency for students with poorer grades to give boredom with courses as a reason for dropping out: 23 percent of the students who cite boredom have undergraduate grade averages of C− or lower, compared with only 17 percent who do not give this reason. Nevertheless, fully 18 percent of the students who give boredom as a reason for leaving college actually have average grades of B or higher.

A somewhat stronger association with undergraduate academic achievement is shown for the item "inability to take desired courses or programs." Among those giving this reason for leaving college, 28 percent have grades of C− or lower, compared with only 18 percent of those who do not give this reason. There is no significant relationship between the student's undergraduate gradepoint average and the tendency to give dissatisfaction with requirements or regulations as a reason for leaving college.

These findings suggest that the academic programs of many undergraduate institutions fail to capture the interest of substantial numbers of students, including some of the highest achievers. Boredom with courses may be an important factor in the decision of many able students to leave college.

Further analyses of reasons for leaving college yield some interesting differences between blacks and whites. In general, whites are more likely than blacks to check more than one reason. Among the reasons showing the greatest differences between whites and blacks are boredom with courses (33 percent of whites versus 18 percent of blacks), dissatisfaction with requirements or regulations (23 percent versus 11 percent), and change in career plans (21 percent versus 11 percent). Blacks are much more likely than whites to check financial difficulties (43 percent versus 27 percent) and marriage (27 percent versus 21 percent). The substantial number of blacks who report leaving college for financial reasons is consistent with earlier findings (see Astin, King, Light, and Richardson, 1974; Bayer and Boruch, 1969), which showed clearly that, compared with whites, blacks came from much poorer families and expressed substantially greater concern over their financial problems at the time they first entered college.

Although the reasons for leaving college given by the stopouts largely resemble those given by the dropouts, some notable exceptions occur. Stopouts, for example, are much more likely than dropouts to give illness or accident as a reason for leaving college. This difference is especially large among women: the percentage of female stopouts giving this reason is more than twice that of dropouts (16 percent versus 7 percent, respectively). Stopouts are also more likely to report disciplinary troubles as a reason for leaving college. (This difference is limited to the men, among whom 4.3 percent of the stopouts, compared with only 1.7 percent of the dropouts, report that disciplinary problems are a factor.) Stopouts are significantly *less* likely than dropouts to give any one of the following reasons for leaving college: marriage, dissatisfaction with requirements or regulations, and inability to take desired courses or programs. These differences further confirm the conceptual distinction between dropouts and stopouts: whereas stopouts are more likely to leave college for temporary or transitory reasons (illness, accident, disciplinary suspension), dropouts are more likely to report fundamental dissatisfaction with their colleges.

Current Status of Dropouts

Determining the proportion of dropouts currently employed, looking for a job, or not looking for a job provides a broader context in which to interpret the definitions of dropouts, stopouts, and persisters. Because a number of dropouts are married and because they give marriage so frequently as a reason for leaving college, students' current employment status in fall 1972 was tabulated separately by sex and marital status. Table 4 shows the results.

The employment patterns for married dropouts reveal striking differences between the sexes. In general, those differences correspond to traditional sex roles. Whereas better than 90 percent of the married men are employed full time and only 2 percent are unemployed and not looking for work, only 49 percent of the married women are employed full time, with an additional 33

Table 4.

EMPLOYMENT STATUS OF DROPOUTS BY SEX AND MARITAL STATUS (Fall 1972)
(Percentages)

Employment Status	Married		Not Married	
	Men (N = 64,934)	Women (N = 66,362)	Men (N = 108,021)	Women (N = 47,628)
Full-time job	91.3	49.2	72.4	75.8
Part-time job	2.9	12.4	8.5	7.9
Looking for job: unsatisfactory offers	1.5	2.1	5.8	3.9
Looking for job: no offers	.4	2.3	4.4	2.9
Not looking for job	2.1	33.5	7.4	7.6
No response	1.8	.4	1.6	2.1

percent unemployed and not looking for work. Traditional sex roles are also reflected in the much larger proportion of women who work at part-time jobs (12 percent versus 3 percent for men). Married men, it would appear, have largely accepted their traditional roles as breadwinners, whereas one in three married women dropouts has apparently settled for the role of homemaker.

Some of the results for unmarried dropouts are in striking contrast to those for married dropouts. Slightly *more* unmarried women than unmarried men are employed full time, with no significant difference in the proportions of the two sexes unemployed and not looking for work. In contrast to married dropouts, single women dropouts are actually *less* likely than men to hold part-time jobs. It seems that, as long as dropouts remain single, traditional sex roles in employment status do not appear.

Is it possible that the act of dropping out may force married dropouts into more traditional sex roles? To examine this hypothesis, the employment status of those *persisters* who were not currently enrolled in either undergraduate or graduate study was tabulated. This group, which includes approximately 41 percent of the total population of students who started college in 1968, comprises those who completed the bachelor's degree but who did not go immediately into graduate or professional school. Theoretically, one might expect most students from this large group to be employed or looking for work at the time of the follow-up.

As it turned out, those married baccalaureate recipients who do not enroll in postgraduate study show employment patterns that resemble those for the married dropouts, although the sex differences are markedly attenuated. Thus, the percentages of married bachelor's degree recipients employed full time are 78 percent and 63 percent for men and women, respectively. The percentages unemployed and not looking for work are 6 percent and 11 percent for men and women, respectively. Among the unmarried degree-holders not enrolled in postgraduate study, significantly more women are employed full time (65 percent versus 55 percent for men). Among these unmarried baccalaureate recipients, a much larger proportion of men than women are unemployed and not looking for work (13 percent versus 7 percent). Apparently, single men are somewhat more likely than single women to take time off from school and work after they receive the baccalaureate degree.

The fact that such a high proportion of married women with degrees are employed full time and that such a relatively low proportion are unemployed and not looking for work suggests that the effects of marriage on a woman's career development are substantially reduced if she can avoid dropping out and can complete the baccalaureate degree. Whether these differences in the employment status of married persisters and married dropouts will continue in the years ahead can only be answered with longer term longitudinal studies.

2

PREDICTING
WHICH FRESHMEN
WILL DROP OUT

Since the primary aim of this study is prediction rather than de-scription, an important first step is to identify which personal characteristics of college entrants predict dropping out. Previous studies (A. W. Astin, 1971, 1972a; H. S. Astin, 1970; Astin and Panos, 1969; Cope, 1969; DeVecchio, 1972; Newman, 1965; Sum-merskill, 1962; Trent and Medsker, 1967) suggest that a number of student background characteristics may be predictive: ability, secondary school grades, socioeconomic status, and educational aspirations, as well as the students' own predictions about their chances of finishing college. The ability to estimate, on the basis of these indicators, any given student's chances of dropping out is of potential value to all three groups of decision-makers: students, institutional administrators, and educational policy-makers.

Students, of course, have a vested interest in knowing what their chances of completing college really are. This knowledge may influence their institutional choice or possibly even their decision to attend college. Institutional administrators and educational policy-makers need such information to obtain relatively unbiased estimates of the probable impact of policy alternatives. One major purpose of the analyses reported in this chapter is to develop for each student a measure of "dropout-proneness." The measures are used in subsequent chapters to assess the impact of alternative environments and decisions. A hypothetical example illustrates the importance of being able to assess the student's initial likelihood of dropping out. In evaluating the impact of scholarships on students' persistence in college, for instance, one crude approach would be simply to compare the dropout rates of students who do and do not receive scholarship aid. If it turns out that those with aid are less likely to drop out, one might be tempted to conclude that scholarships increase students' chances of staying in college. Policy-makers might then be prompted to believe that scholarships represent a useful device to reduce college attrition rates.

The problem with such an analysis is that simple differences in dropout rates between scholarship recipients and nonrecipients may have nothing to do with receiving aid, as such. It is not unreasonable to assume, for example, that those who receive scholarships may be less dropout-prone in the first place because of greater ability, motivation, and so on. However, if it were possible to develop independent estimates of each student's proneness to dropping out (utilizing data on ability, past achievements, family background, race, age, sex, educational aspirations, and so forth), one could obtain a less biased estimate of the effects of scholarships by determining whether the scholarship recipients' actual dropout rate is different from their *expected* rate based on these personal characteristics. Thus if the actual dropout rate of scholarship recipients is lower than that of nonrecipients and yet the two groups' expected rates are about the same, such information would be evidence that scholarship aid does increase students' chances of persisting in college. Conversely, if the actual rate for recipients is higher than their expected rate (and the actual rate for nonrecipients lower than their expected rate), one could conclude that scholarships increase dropout chances. If the expected rates for the two groups differ by about the same amount as their actual rates, the conclusion would

be that scholarships have no impact one way or the other on persistence.

Method

The initial task was to determine how dropping out is related
to the information provided by the students on the entering freshman questionnaire and to the college admissions test scores provided
by the institutions. Ability test scores (SAT verbal plus mathematical and ACT composite) were converted to a common scale using a
procedure described by Astin (1971). Students for whom no scores
were available (about 20 percent of the total sample) were assigned
the mean score for their fellow students at the institution (see
Table 3–6 in Astin, 1971). Also included as possible dropout predictors were items from the 1968 freshman questionnaire: sex, age,
high school grades, extracurricular achievements in high school
(such as winning a varsity letter, editing the school paper), highest
academic degree planned (each degree scored as a separate predictor), student's concern about finances, educational level of the
student's parents, parental family income, racial background (each
of five categories scored as a separate variable), religion in which the
student was reared (five separate variables), current religious preference (five separate variables), student's rating of the academic standards of the high school, rank in high school graduating class, type of
town in which student grew up (five separate variables), study
habits (26 separate variables), expectations about what will happen
during college (15 separate variables), intended career choice,
probable field of study, and daily activities. Because of the large
number of items in the last three groups of variables (career choice,
major field, and daily activities), the only items selected for analysis
were those that had been shown previously to relate to dropping out
(see Astin, 1972a). All in all, 110 student personal characteristics
were analyzed.

A preliminary screening to determine the importance of
these 110 variables was conducted with linear stepwise multiple
regression analyses. The original sample of 41,356 students was
reduced to 38,703 by eliminating all students who did not aspire to
at least the bachelor's degree when they entered college in 1968
(see Chapter One). Using every fourth subject ($N = 9,750$) to

reduce computing costs, two separate regression analyses were conducted. Each analysis employed a dichotomous dependent variable: dropout versus nondropout. In the first analysis, nondropouts included both persisters and stopouts. In the second analysis, only the persisters were considered nondropouts while the dropout category included both stopouts and dropouts. These alternative definitions were employed to see whether the results would be significantly altered by placing the stopouts in one category rather than the other. (As it turned out, the high degree of similarity between dropouts and stopouts resulted in a decision to combine these two groups for most of the subsequent predictive analyses.)

In these initial analyses, the 110 independent or predictor variables were allowed to enter the regression analysis in a stepwise fashion until no additional predictor was capable of adding significantly ($p < .01$) to the prediction of dropping out. Fifty-three of the 110 student personal variables contributed significantly to the prediction of dropping out in one or both analyses. Most of these variables entered into both analyses. (In subsequent chapters it will be shown that the accuracy of these predictions based on entering student characteristics can be increased significantly by adding data on financial aid, work status, place of residence, and college characteristics.)

Next, these 53 student variables were used as predictors in a series of regression analyses performed separately on selected subgroups of students. Because of the current interest in the educational development of both women and minorities, these analyses were performed separately for four groups of students: nonblack men, nonblack women, blacks enrolling in black colleges, and blacks enrolling in white colleges. (Excluded from these four groups are 421 students who either gave no race or who were nonblacks enrolled in black colleges.) The actual unweighted number of students in each group was:

Nonblack men	18,069
Nonblack women	17,074
Blacks in black colleges	1,378
Blacks in white colleges	1,761

While it might be informative to perform separate analyses for minorities other than blacks, the numbers are too small to produce stable results (266 Chicanos, 45 Puerto Ricans, 235 American Indians, and 1,120 Orientals). For simplicity, nonblack students will be called whites, although it should be kept in mind that these other minority groups account for about 4 percent of the two white samples. The weighted population estimates of percentages of drop-outs and stopouts in the four groups are:

	Stopouts	Dropouts
White men	11	26
White women	8	23
Blacks in black colleges	11	26
Blacks in white colleges	13	37

Although these data suggest that the stopout and dropout rates of the first three groups are quite close, the rates for the last group—blacks attending white colleges—are substantially higher. The higher attrition rate appears to be attributable in part to the effect of attending a white college, rather than to differences in initial dropout-proneness between blacks in white colleges and blacks in black colleges (see Chapter Seven).

The two regression analyses described above were repeated separately for each of the four student groups, using only the 52 variables identified in the initial analysis. (One of the original 53—race: black—was not used because the formation of the four groups eliminated it as a variable.) The final equation from each stepwise regression analysis was used to develop an estimate of dropout-proneness for each student.

An actual example from one of the four groups—white women—illustrates how these measures of dropout-proneness are actually derived. (For this example, the definition of dropout includes both dropouts and stopouts.) In this analysis, the first variable entering the regression equation is the student's average grade in high school. On the freshman questionnaire, the student was asked to mark one of eight alternatives: D, C, C+, B−, B, B+, A−, and A or A+. For the regression analyses, these responses are scored on an eight-point scale: D = 1, . . . A or A+ = 8. If this were the only measure of student personal characteristics, the regression analysis would, of course, end after one step, and estimates of dropout-proneness would be based on the regression equation that results from this one-step analysis.

Suppose one wishes to obtain estimates of dropout-proneness for two students: Smith and Jones. Jones is a borderline student with a C average in high school. Smith is a superior student whose grade average was A. To obtain the estimates, the regression equation is based only on high school grades. The general form of any regression equation that utilizes a single predictor is:

$$\text{predicted score} = \text{constant} + \left[\text{weight} \times \text{predictor}\right]$$

(chances in 100 of dropping out) (high school grades)

If high school grades alone are used to predict dropping out, the regression equation has these values: constant = 68.03; weight = −7.137.

Applying these weights in the regression for Jones (whose C average is scored as 2) provides the following equation:

Jones's chances in 100 of dropping out =

$$68.03 + \left[-7.137 \times 2\right]$$

Jones's chances in 100 of dropping out =

54 (rounded)

Smith, whose A average receives a score of 8, provides the following equation:

Smith's chances in 100 of dropping out =

$$68.03 \times \left[-7.137 \times 8\right]$$

Smith's chances in 100 of dropping out =

11 (rounded)

Now suppose there is not one but two predictor variables: high school grades plus SAT scores. Assume that Jones's SAT scores are quite low, with a total on both verbal and mathematical of 700. Smith, on the other hand, has a relatively high total verbal and mathematical score of 1300. The general form of a regression equation that utilizes two or more predictors is:

predicted score = constant +

$$\left[\begin{array}{c}\text{weight for}\\\text{first}\\\text{variable}\end{array} \times \begin{array}{c}\text{first}\\\text{variable}\end{array}\right] + \left[\begin{array}{c}\text{weight for}\\\text{second}\\\text{variable}\end{array} \times \begin{array}{c}\text{second}\\\text{variable}\end{array}\right]$$

If high school grades and SAT composite scores are used in combination to predict dropping out among white women, the regression equation contains these values: constant = 99.420; weight for high school grades = −5.482; weight for SAT composite score = −.03944. The formula would then be:

chances in 100 = 99.420 +

$$\left[-5.482 \times \text{high school grades}\right] + \left[-.03944 \times \text{SAT composite}\right]$$

Applying weights to estimate Jones's chances of dropping out and using her high school grade score of 2 (C average) and her SAT composite score of 700 provides the regression equation:

Jones's chances in 100 of dropping out =

$$99.420 + \left[-5.48 \times 2\right] + \left[-.03944 \times 700\right]$$

Jones's chances in 100 of dropping out =

61 (rounded)

Notice that with the additional knowledge of Jones's low test scores, the estimated chance of dropping out is somewhat higher (61 in 100 compared with 54 in 100 with only high school grades). Of course, if Jones's SAT scores were quite high, say, 1200, the estimate of her chances of dropping out would be substantially lower (41 in 100).

As for Smith, when her high school grade score of 8 (A average) and her SAT composite score of 1300 are plugged into the same formula, the results are:

$$\text{Smith's chances in 100 of dropping out} =$$
$$99.420 + \left[-5.482 \times 8\right] + \left[-.03944 \times 1300\right]$$

Smith's chances in 100 of dropping out =

4 (rounded)

Notice that each additional student variable provides a more precise estimate of the student's chances of dropping out. Thus, a total of 37 of the 52 student predictors turn out to carry some statistically significant weight in the estimation of dropout-proneness among white women. The number of predictors entering the equations for the other three groups are: white men (40), blacks in black colleges (31), and blacks in white colleges (43).[1] As with most regression analyses that use numerous variables, each successive predictor adds substantially less to predictive accuracy than the previous one. Even though the final 20 or 25 predictors in each additional analysis add only a small amount of precision to the estimates, all variables that contribute anything of statistical significance ($p < .05$) have been included to exert the fullest possible control over initial differences in characteristics among college entrants.

For students or college administrators who wish to obtain their own estimates of dropout-proneness, the worksheets at the end of the book contain the complete regression formulas for all four groups and give the 52 predictors in detail.

The significance of the 52 student characteristics that entered into each regression analysis is discussed below under six general headings: academic background and ability, family background, educational aspirations, study habits, expectations about the college, and other student characteristics. Different categories of variables

---

[1] The corresponding multiple correlations after the final step in each analysis are: white men ($R = .379$); white women ($R = .382$); blacks in black colleges ($R = .386$); and blacks in white colleges ($R = .540$).

will be considered in descending order of importance, beginning with the most predictive variables.

Academic Background

A substantial body of research has shown clearly that the student's academic performance in secondary school is a major predictor of college attrition. The measures used in most studies have included the student's average high school grade, rank in high school graduating class, and academic ability as measured by college admissions test scores. These measures have been negatively related to dropping out of college in such diverse settings as junior colleges (DeVecchio, 1972; Eagle, 1973; MacMillan, 1970), public universities (Chase, 1970; Cope, 1969, 1970), and private colleges (Hannah, 1971), and for such varied groups as probationary freshmen (Morrisey, 1971), high ability students (Astin, 1964; Hill, 1966), blacks (Baber and Caple, 1970; Mack, 1973), and engineering students (Miller and Twyman, 1967). Moreover, these same measures of academic ability and past academic achievement have been positively related to student persistence in several national studies involving large institutional samples (Astin, 1971, 1972a; Astin and Panos, 1969; Bayer, 1968).

The analyses here deal with four measures of the student's academic background which proved to be significantly related to dropping out: average high school grade, rank in high school class (scored on a six-point scale: top 1 percent, top 10 percent, top quarter, second quarter, third quarter, fourth quarter), college admissions test scores, and student's academic rating of the high school (scored on a five-point scale: very high, fairly high, about average, probably below average, definitely below average). Each measure contributes significantly to the prediction equation for each student group (white men, white women, blacks in black colleges, blacks in white colleges).

High School Grades. That the student's high school grades would prove the most consistently potent predictor of college attrition[2] is not surprising, considering that prior research has con-

---

[2] The strength or "potency" of any predictor (class rank, for example)

sistently shown that high school grades are the best predictor of college grades. To illustrate the importance of high school grades in predicting a student's chances of dropping out, the four groups have been combined in Table 5 to present a composite picture of this relationship.

Table 5.

HIGH SCHOOL GRADES RELATED TO PERSISTENCE

Average Grade in High School	Persisters (Percent)	Stopouts (Percent)	Dropouts (Percent)	Weighted Population (Number)
A or A+	87	6	7	61,253
A—	82	7	11	112,801
B+	77	8	15	200,140
B	66	11	23	278,059
B—	62	13	25	181,483
C+	52	13	35	179,343
C	44	13	43	159,830

These data show clearly that students' chances either of stopping out or dropping out of college increase consistently as their high school grades decrease. The fact that stopping out and dropping out show similar patterns suggests that stopouts resemble dropouts more than they do persisters. Under these circumstances, any dichotomous measure of dropping out should probably combine stopouts with dropouts rather than with the persisters. (Several additional findings presented below confirm this assumption.)

Rank in High School Class. Another measure of the student's

is assessed in terms of the percentage difference in the estimate of dropout-proneness which would result if the student had a high rather than a low score on that predictor (for example, class rank of "top 1 percent" versus "fourth quarter"). To compute this difference for any variable, multiply the regression weight for that variable (see Worksheets at the end of this book) separately by extreme scores on the variable and compare the resulting proportions (multiply the difference by 100 to get percentage).

academic achievement in high school—rank in class—also contributes independently to the prediction of dropping out, although the
relationship is not as strong as the one for grades. The single exception to this trend occurs among blacks attending white colleges.
For these students, rank in high school class is a more potent
predictor of dropping out than average high school grade.

College Admissions Tests. While the students' composite
scores on the SAT and ACT contribute significantly to the
accuracy of estimates of dropout-proneness, the predictive strength
of these test scores is consistently smaller than that of high school
grades. This difference is particularly pronounced among black
students. For both groups of blacks, SAT or ACT scores contribute
only marginally to the prediction. One possible explanation for this
result may be the smaller variation in test scores shown by black
students (the standard deviations in the college admissions test
scores for both black groups are substantially lower than the standard
deviations for the two white groups).

Academic Rating of High School. The students' ratings of
the academic quality of their high schools add significantly to the
precision of the estimate of dropout-proneness in all four groups. In
all cases, dropping out is associated with a relatively low high
school rating. Although earlier attempts to improve the prediction
of college grades by "adjusting" students' high school grades through
the use of some high school "quality" measure have proved largely
unsuccessful (Lindquist, 1963), these findings suggest that students
themselves are able to recognize differences in the academic quality of
high schools. Two earlier studies (Cope, 1972; DeVecchio, 1972) report that high school *size* is positively related to college persistence. If
the larger high schools also tend to have more stringent grading
standards, then the students from those high schools may tend to
rate their academic standards somewhat higher than do students
attending smaller high schools. These ratings would, in turn, serve
as a kind of adjustment to the high school grades and class rank as
predictors of college attrition.

Family Background

The battery of predictors included several groups of family
background measures: religion, parental education and income,

race, and type of home town. Several items from each group carried substantial weight in estimating dropout-proneness.

Religion. Measures of the religion of the students' parents and of the students' own religious preference are related to proneness to dropping out in all four groups. Although these relationships are somewhat complex, the results are generally similar for all groups.

Entering college freshmen who indicated "none" or "other" as their religious preference are most likely to drop out of college. Students who checked "Jewish" as their religious preference are least likely to drop out, followed by students who checked "Catholic." These relationships become more complex, however, when the religion of the students' parents is also considered.

The most dropout-prone students are those whose parents are Protestant but who themselves indicate no religious preference. When other factors are held constant, the expected dropout rate for this group is about 40 percent, compared with an expected rate of only 19 percent among the least dropout-prone group: students with Jewish parents who also indicate that their religious preference is Jewish. The expected rate for Catholic students with Catholic parents is about 26 percent, while the expected rate for Protestant students with Protestant parents is about 30 percent.

These relationships between religious background and preference and persistence in college occur *independently* of factors such as ability, degree plans, and other family background variables.[3] Indeed, when other student characteristics are not controlled, the relationship between no religious preference and persistence is positive. Highly able students tend to give no religious preference more often than less able students. However, once these ability measures are considered in the multiple regression equation, having no religious preference turns out to be negatively associated with persistence. In other words, students who enter college expressing no religious preference are more likely to drop out than students of comparable ability and background who express a preference. (This finding highlights the usefulness of a technique such as multiple

---

[3] The importance of various predictors is based on regression weights from equations used to estimate dropout-proneness (see Worksheets). These weights reflect the independent contribution of each predictor when it is considered jointly with all other predictors.

regression analysis, which can deal simultaneously with numerous predictor measures.)

The tendency for Jewish students to show greater persistence in college than non-Jewish students has been reported in several earlier studies (Astin, 1971; Astin and Panos, 1969; Newman, 1965). That having Jewish parents should be a positive factor in college persistence invites explanation. Parents of one religious persuasion, for example, may be more likely to exert pressure on the student to stay in college than parents of another religious persuasion. Another possibility is that Jewish students possess certain subtle personal attributes not reflected in the various measures of ability, motivation, and family background. Still another possible influence is the effect of particular college characteristics. The relatively high persistence rate of Catholics, for example, may be due to the differential holding power of Catholic versus non-Catholic colleges (see Chapter Six). Since students from Catholic backgrounds are disproportionately concentrated in Catholic colleges, this college effect would show up in an analysis as an effect of a religious background variable.

The tendency for students with no religious preference to drop out of college frequently has also been reported in earlier studies (Astin, 1972a; Astin and Panos, 1969; Newman, 1965). Several other studies of dropouts suggest that to express no religious preference may be a sign of independence and nonconformity. College persistence is relatively low, for example, among students who are autonomous, independent, nonconforming, complex, and critical of their parents (Astin, 1964; Cohen, Brawer, and Connor, 1969; DeVecchio, 1972; Johnson, 1970; Newman, 1965; Snyder, 1967; Trent and Medsker, 1967). While the battery of student predictor variables does not include measures of personality as such, the "nonconformity" hypothesis is supported by the relationships between dropping out and such factors as study habits and smoking behavior (see below).

Parental Income and Education. With the current national and state emphasis on improvement of student financial aid programs, the income level of college students' parents has become an item of major interest. When other variables are ignored, family income (determined by students' best estimates) shows a clear-cut relationship to dropping out:

	Dropouts, Percent
Less than $ 4,000	31
$ 4,000 – 5,999	29
$ 6,000 – 7,999	27
$ 8,000 – 9,999	27
$10,000 – 14,999	24
$15,000 – 19,999	23
$20,000 – 24,999	16
$25,000 – 29,999	18
$30,000 or more	14

A negative association between parental income and college attrition has also been reported by several earlier investigators (Cope, 1969; Trapp, Pailthorp, and Cope, 1971). However, when family income is included in the regression analyses with other measures of family background and student ability and motivation, it fails to add anything over and above the contribution of these other variables. In short, the relationship between family income and college attrition appears to be mediated by such factors as student ability, parental education, and student concern about finances. The greater dropout-proneness of students from low-income families is attributable to their less educated parents, lesser ability and lower motivation, and greater concern about finances.

The educational level of each parent was measured on a six-point scale (1 = grammar school . . . 6 = graduate degree). Both measures carry negative weights in the prediction of college attrition, a result reported in several earlier studies (Astin, 1972a; Astin and Panos, 1969; Chase, 1970; Cope, 1970; Cohen, Brawer, and Connor, 1969; Trent and Medsker, 1967). Since parental educational level contributes to the estimate of dropout-proneness independently of other student variables, it cannot be argued that students of more educated parents drop out less often merely because they are more able academically. It seems likely that the more educated parents exert stronger pressure on students to stay in college than the less educated parents. Also, a student may be deterred from dropping out by the knowledge that his or her parents completed college.

Students' concern about finances as scored on a three-point scale—no concern ("I am confident that I will have sufficient funds"), some concern ("but I will probably have enough funds"), major concern ("not sure I will be able to complete college")— carries substantial weight in the regressions for two groups: white women and blacks in black colleges. This item carries a nonsignificant weight for men and a slight negative association with dropping out for blacks in white colleges.

These findings suggest several possibilities. That financial concern should be related to dropping out for women but not for men may indicate that women are more likely to let financial considerations influence their decision to remain in or to leave college. The contrasting results for blacks in white colleges and blacks in black colleges may be due to the differing amounts of financial aid available in these two types of colleges. Also, in the white colleges, blacks receive a relatively large share of the financial aid (see Chapter Three).

Race. Although it was not practical to perform separate regression analyses for racial groups other than blacks and non-blacks, one should note the overall dropout rate for students in each group:

	Dropouts, Percent
Orientals	19
Whites	24
Blacks	29
American Indians	31
Chicanos	31

Whites and Orientals clearly have the lowest dropout rates, whereas Chicanos and American Indians have the highest rate. The data suggest that the high rate for Chicanos is largely attributable to their high concentration in two-year colleges. (This concentration is probably due to the fact that most Chicanos live in the Western states, where much higher proportions of students attend community colleges than in other sections of the country.) Since attending a community college appears to reduce a student's chances of persisting (see Chapter Six), the high concentration of Chicanos in the two-year colleges increases their overall dropout rate substantially. In fact, within the four-year colleges and universities the Chicano dropout rate is actually lower than that of whites (14 percent versus 18 percent). The four-year college and university dropout rates for the other three ethnic groups are: Orientals, 10; blacks, 23; and American Indians, 28.

In the regression analyses for nonblack men and nonblack women, being Oriental is associated with staying in college. Being Oriental reduces the estimate of dropout chances by about 7 percent for men and 10 percent for women. Again, continuing parental encouragement to stay in college represents a likely explanation for this result.

Home Town. The follow-up questionnaire asked where the student lived most of the time while growing up. Each of the five alternatives (farm, small town, moderate-sized town or city, suburb of large city, large city) was scored as a separate dichotomous variable for the regression analysis (farm versus all others, small town versus all others, and so on). Growing up in a small town is most consistently related to dropping out within the four groups, a finding reported in two earlier studies (Cope, 1972; Newman, 1965). Growing up in a large city or suburb is associated with dropping out among men but with persistence among women.

The association between dropping out and growing up in a small town is subject to a variety of explanations, the "culture shock" phenomenon being among the most likely. Another possibility is that students from small towns are more likely to attend colleges which encourage dropping out than students who grow up in larger towns. This possibility will be explored in Chapter Seven.

Educational Aspirations

Although students who did not aspire to at least a bachelor's degree at matriculation have been excluded from this study, the student's degree aspirations are still related to college persistence and attrition. Students who aspire to a doctorate or professional degree are the least likely to drop out of college, while students who aspire to a bachelor's or "other" degree (this latter group, about 3 percent of the students, was combined with the bachelor's group earlier; see Table 1) have the greatest chance of dropping out.

Perhaps the simplest way to illustrate the relative importance of degree plans is to contrast the regression weights of various degrees in terms of what they add to the student's estimated probability of dropping out. For white men, aspiring to a master's rather than a doctoral or professional degree adds about 5 percent to the chances of dropping out. Aspiring to a bachelor's degree adds another 7 percent, and aspiring to "other" degree adds another 12 percent. Thus, the difference between the estimated dropout probability associated with aspiring to a Ph.D. or professional degree and that associated with "other" degree is approximately 24 percent. For white women, the pattern is similar except that aspiring to a bachelor's rather than a doctoral or professional degree adds only about 4 percent to the dropout chances, and aspiring to a master's degree is associated with a lower probability of dropping out (about 3 percent less) than aspiring to a doctorate or professional degree.

Another index of students' educational aspirations is the intended field of study at time of college entrance. Although field of study, as such, does not contribute to the accuracy of prediction in the multiple correlational analysis, it is useful to explore the attrition rates for students in different majors. For this analysis, students from all four groups have been combined and the dropout rates tabulated. Because two-year colleges are more likely than four-year colleges to offer certain fields of study, these analyses have been performed separately for both types of institutions.

The fields of study with the highest dropout rates in *both* two- and four-year institutions are secretarial studies, forestry, electronics, and nursing. With the possible exception of forestry, careers in these fields can be pursued without a baccalaureate degree. While students entering two-year colleges are more likely to major in these fields than students entering four-year colleges and universities, the dropout rates for students in these fields in two-year colleges are much larger (56 percent to 74 percent) than in four-year colleges and universities (25 percent to 33 percent).

Fields with the lowest dropout rates show no consistent pattern in relation to two- and four-year institutions. In the two-year colleges these fields include home economics (23 percent), library science (25 percent), prelaw (26 percent), business administration (30 percent), and history (30 percent). In the four-year colleges and universities, they include military science (7 percent), pre-medical (9 percent), predental (10 percent), earth science (10 percent), biochemistry (10 percent), biology (10 percent), chemical engineering (11 percent), and political science (11 percent). (For a complete listing of dropout rates in 66 fields of study, see Astin, 1975.)

Study Habits

Eleven of the items associated with study habits ("During the *past year* in school, how often did the following statements apply to you?") contribute significantly to estimates of dropout-proneness. Of these, three relate to college persistence: "turned in assigned work on time," "did my homework at the same time everyday," "made careless mistakes on a test." The first two items relate to students' ability to schedule their time and organize their work to meet a deadline for assignments. On the surface, the third item seems surprising. One possible explanation for the relationship is that "careless mistakes," in contrast to mistakes that result from lack of knowledge or incompetence, are more likely to be made by the superior student. Also, admitting to careless mistakes reflects an ability to be self-critical which may be more characteristic of better students.

While the study-habit items relating to college persistence are surprising, several of these items relating to dropping out provide even more surprises: "kept my desk or study place neat," "did unrequired work for extra credit," "carefully went over diagrams or tables in the textbook," "was too bored to study," "had trouble concentrating on assignments," "studied with the radio or record player on," "failed to complete a homework assignment on time." Perhaps most unexpected is the item on unrequired work for extra credit. Upon closer inspection, however, it seems likely that students are frequently pressured into extra work because their regular course work has been poor. "Extra credit" becomes a device to salvage an otherwise failing grade. Equally puzzling is "kept my desk or study place neat." One possibility, of course, is that students who do little or no homework keep their study place neater than students who regularly do their homework. The third unexpected item—carefully going over diagrams or tables—also presents interpretative challenges. Perhaps the key here is "carefully." Students who find it difficult to interpret diagrams or tables may spend more time going over the minute details in an attempt to comprehend them.

Whatever the proper explanation for the presence of these first three items, they provide some potentially important clues for counselors and researchers interested in pursuing in-depth studies of academic achievement and college persistence. The last four items related to dropping out are consistent with more popular conceptions of the poor student: boredom, difficulty in concentrating, studying with outside distractions, and not completing homework.

Expectations About College

The freshman questionnaire asked students to estimate the chances that certain outcomes would occur. Of particular value, of course, are the students' self-predictions about dropping out. Table 6 shows students' estimates of their chances of dropping out temporarily or permanently, separately for two-year colleges and four-year colleges and universities. Few students (less than 1 percent) thought they had a "very good chance" of dropping out, either temporarily or permanently. In fact, two-thirds said they had "no chance" of dropping out. Two-year-college freshmen students are somewhat *less* likely than freshmen in four-year colleges and universities to think they will drop out, either permanently or temporarily—a surprising fact, considering that their actual dropout chances are substantially higher. Two-year college students, it seems, have unrealistic expectations about their chances of finishing.

How accurate are these self-estimates of the odds on leaving college before graduation? Table 7 suggests that they are only

Table 6.

STUDENTS' ESTIMATES OF DROPOUT CHANCES
(Weighted National Ns and Percentages)

| 1968 Estimate of Dropout Chances | Students Initially Entering | | | |
| | Four-Year Colleges and Universities | | Two-Year Colleges | |
	N	Percentage	N	Percentage
Temporarily				
No chance	401,946	44.4	149,358	53.8
Very little chance	419,926	46.4	110,233	39.7
Some chance	73,392	8.1	15,716	5.7
Very good chance	9,044	1.0	2,189	.8
Permanently				
No chance	564,161	62.4	193,309	69.7
Very little chance	297,710	32.9	76,824	27.7
Some chance	38,498	4.3	6,499	2.3
Very good chance	3,916	.4	856	.3

moderately accurate. Among students who enter four-year colleges saying they have "no chance" of dropping out, most (74.6 percent) are persisters, but one in six (16.0 percent) becomes a dropout. Among four-year college entrants who say their chances of dropping out permanently are "very good," the dropout rate is twice as high: 33.5 percent.

Students' estimates are also positively related to their chances of stopping out, although the relationship between estimates and dropping out is stronger. Apparently, the distinction between "temporarily" and "permanently" is not relevant in predicting stopping out versus dropping out.

In short, Tables 6 and 7 suggest some realism in the students' own estimate of their dropout chances. Although the large majority of students indicate when they enter college that there is

Table 7.

ACCURACY OF STUDENTS' ESTIMATES OF DROPOUT CHANCES
(Weighted National Percentages)

1968 Estimate of Dropout Chances	Students Initially Entering					
	Four-Year Colleges and Universities			Two-Year Colleges		
	Persisters	Stopouts	Dropouts	Persisters	Stopouts	Dropouts
Temporarily						
No chance	74.7	9.4	15.9	45.8	12.9	41.3
Very little chance	71.0	9.7	19.2	43.3	14.1	42.6
Some chance	59.9	12.2	27.9	23.1	23.6	53.4
Very good chance	50.8	12.9	36.3	12.1	20.4	67.5
Permanently						
No chance	74.6	9.4	16.0	43.7	13.7	42.6
Very little chance	67.7	10.4	21.9	42.6	14.8	42.6
Some chance	60.0	10.1	29.9	40.0	18.7	41.3
Very good chance	52.4	14.1	33.5	—*	—*	—*

* Ns too small to compute reliable percentages.

"no chance" of their dropping out, a substantial proportion—particularly in two-year colleges—actually become dropouts.

In the multiple regression analyses, only the item on temporarily dropping out enters any equation. For white men and blacks in white colleges, the item has a moderate positive weight associated with dropping out.

One self-prediction entering into all four regression analyses is the students' estimate that they will transfer to another college before graduation. In all cases, the regression weight associated with this item is *negative,* indicating that students who begin college with plans to transfer have a better chance of persisting than students without such plans. When these analyses are performed separately for two-year and four-year colleges, the results are somewhat different. Among students entering two-year colleges, plans to transfer are, not surprisingly, even more strongly associated with persistence since transferring is a necessary step for two-year college entrants who wish to obtain a baccalaureate degree. Among students entering four-year colleges, however, plans to transfer are negatively associated with persistence, a finding discussed fully in Chapter Six.

Another self-prediction that merits attention is "get married while in college." Positive responses to this item are related to dropping out. The relationship for women is substantial, while the relationship for men is nonsignificant. Here again is evidence that the negative impact of marriage on student persistence in college is much greater for women than for men.

Other Characteristics

One item in the list of student activities in high school—"smoked cigarettes"—has pronounced relationships to attrition in the final regression equations for all four groups. This effect is especially large among both groups of black students. Thus, in estimating dropout probabilities from the regression weights, the black student who smokes "frequently" has a dropout probability about 20 percent greater than the student who smokes "not at all." The comparable difference for white men is only about 5 percent and for white women about 7 percent.

While the association between smoking and dropping out of college has been noted by other investigators (Dvorak, 1967; Pumroy, 1967), the reasons for the association are not clearly understood. Smoking may be a symptom of rebelliousness and non-conformity—traits directly associated with dropping out. Smoking may directly interfere with concentration or produce physiological stress that interferes with the ability to study or to conform to the academic and social demands of college. Whatever the explanation, the magnitude of this association, particularly for black students, suggests that the relationships among smoking, academic performance, and college persistence may be fertile ground for future interdisciplinary research focused on physiological as well as psychological and behavioral variables.

Another item associated with college attrition is age. Older students, particularly older women, are more likely to drop out than students of traditional entry age (17–19). (The proportion of older students in the sample is relatively small: 3 percent are 20 or 21, and 5 percent are over 21.) This finding is consistent with research by Newman (1965), who reported a positive association between age and dropping out, and by Trent and Medsker (1967), who reported that late entrants are more likely to leave college before finishing.

"Won a varsity letter in high school" also carries significant weight in the final regression equation. This item is related to college *persistence* in all groups except black students in black colleges, where it has a nonsignificant weight. Financial aid might be a factor here: in all likelihood, students who win varsity letters in high school are more likely to receive athletic scholarships in college. This additional financial aid, in turn, might represent a positive factor in college persistence (see Chapter Three). Participating in competitive athletics in college (an outcome more likely for those who win high school letters) may involve students more deeply in campus life, reducing the chances that they will leave college. This "involvement" hypothesis will be considered in greater detail in subsequent chapters.

One final student characteristic, marital status at time of matriculation as a freshman, is a significant predictor in the final equations. Although only about 2 percent of the students were married when they started college, this variable carries a substantial weight in the final regression equation for both men and women. The remarkable feature of these weights is that they have opposite signs for the two sexes. Being married at time of college entry increases women's chances of dropping out by about 11 percent, but it *decreases* men's chances by about 8 percent. Here again is striking evidence of the differential effects of marriage on men and women.

Summary

The empirical data reported in this chapter highlight a number of characteristics of entering freshmen that are useful in estimating a given student's chances of dropping out. The most "dropout-prone" freshmen are those with poor academic records in high school, low aspirations, poor study habits, relatively uneducated parents, and small town backgrounds. Dropping out is also associated with being older than most freshmen, having Protestant parents, having no current religious preference, and being a cigarette smoker. Among freshman women, those who are either married or have marriage plans are also more likely to drop out, although among male freshmen being married at the time of college entrance is related to persistence.

The predictors associated with low dropout-proneness produce the opposite pattern. In addition, low dropout-proneness is further associated with being either Jewish or Oriental, with winning varsity letters in high school, and with plans to attend more than one college.

By far the greatest predictive factor is the student's past academic record and academic ability. Next in importance are the student's degree plans at the time of college entrance, religious background, and religious preference, followed by concern about college finances, study habits, and educational attainment of parents. Except for study habits, where there were some unexpected findings, this pattern of predictors is generally consistent with patterns in earlier dropout studies.

Combining these characteristics of entrants by means of

linear multiple regression techniques produces measures of student "dropout-proneness" which are used in subsequent chapters to assess the impact on student persistence of financial aid, work, residence, college characteristics, and student-institutional "fit."

3

IMPACT OF
FINANCIAL AID

Student financial aid programs have provided the basis for much recent public controversy at state and national levels. Debates have focused on a number of issues: How much money should be appropriated? How should available resources be allocated among different types of aid (loans, grants, and work-study programs)? Should aid be administered through the institutions, or should it be available directly to students? Should it be distributed to encourage students to choose particular types of colleges (such as private rather than public)? Should aid be based primarily on financial need, or should other criteria (student aptitude, for example) be used? How is financial need to be defined? How should various forms of aid be packaged for individual students?

Such controversies are difficult to resolve because the *purposes* of student financial aid programs are often not explicit. Among the many possible uses of financial aid programs, the most common are to provide greater access to higher education for students, to assure that students complete their studies, to provide an

47

incentive for students to perform well academically, to reward merit, to influence student choice, and to redistribute wealth.

The use of financial aid to enhance student persistence in college is the focus here. Analyses are designed to determine whether the type and amount of aid and the conditions of its administration have any effect on students' chances of completing college. On the surface, one might expect that *all* forms of financial aid enhance student persistence, since financial problems are among the reasons most commonly given by dropouts for leaving college (Chapter One). If such explanations are valid, any type of financial aid, regardless of source, should reduce the student's chances of leaving college for financial reasons and, thus, positively affect student persistence.

Method

Chapter Two presented a technique for computing the expected probability of dropping out based on each student's personal background characteristics. Since the battery of student predictors includes information on the student's marital status, family education and income, and concern about college finances, presumably these expected probabilities take into account initial differences in financial need. If a particular form of financial aid has a positive effect on student persistence, the actual dropout rate for students who receive that type of aid should be lower than the expected rate based on the students' background characteristics.[1]

One problem with assessing the effects of any single variable, such as financial aid, is that most variables do not occur in isolation; other environmental factors also influence student attrition. For example, students who attend highly selective private colleges are somewhat more likely to receive scholarships or grants than students who attend public community colleges (Astin, King, Light, and

[1] If the expected dropout rates are substantially different, a potential source of bias in such analyses is error in the measures of student characteristics. In certain instances the regression analyses were repeated to determine if conclusions concerning the impact of environmental factors would be different if approximate adjustments for such measurement errors were made. For details, see Astin (1975).

Richardson, 1974). If selective private colleges, in turn, have better holding power on their students than public community colleges, failing to consider college type might produce a spurious "effect" of scholarships or grants which is, in reality, an effect of college type.

To control such biases, the battery of predictors includes not only the student characteristics described in Chapter Two, but also several additional environmental measures covering three general categories: residence, work, and college characteristics. *Residence* predictors include dichotomous measures of three types of residence during the freshman year: home, college dormitory, and private room or apartment. *Work* predictors include four dichotomous measures of work activities during the freshman year: federally sponsored work-study program, other on-campus work, off-campus work, and employment for college credit as part of a departmental program. *College* characteristics include enrollment size, selectivity (an estimate of the average academic ability of the entering freshman; see Astin, 1971), percentage of men students, percentage of undergraduate students, coeducational versus single sex, control (public versus private), and type (three measures: two-year college versus four-year college versus university). Except as noted below, all analyses of the impact of financial aid programs utilize expected dropout probabilities based on these additional environmental characteristics, as well as the student characteristics described earlier.

Even though these additional predictors contribute to less biased estimates of the impact of financial aid, such estimates tend to be somewhat conservative. By controlling all environmental experiences that might be associated with receipt of financial aid (that is, work, residence, and college type) the *shared* effects of aid and these other variables are eliminated. Thus, if scholarship recipients are concentrated more in four-year than in two-year colleges, some (but not all) of the effects of scholarships on attrition will be washed out when college characteristics are included in the calculation of expected dropout probabilities. The greater the degree of overlap (that is, between scholarship aid and these other environmental variables), the more conservative the estimate. The condition under which all the effects of scholarships would be washed out by such an analysis exists only when every scholarship recipient attends just one type of college. This condition never obtains with any of the financial aid measures.

Measures

Undergraduates usually pay their college costs through one or a combination of five different sources of aid: family (parents, spouse, and so on), scholarships, loans, savings, and work. Since savings often come from previous employment, these two categories can be combined. Thus, the principal measures of financial aid cover personal savings and/or employment, parental or other family aid, repayable loan, and scholarship, grant, or other gift. These four items were presented to the entering freshmen of 1968 with the question "Through what source do you intend to finance *the first year* of your undergraduate education?" Students were asked to indicate whether each item was a major source, a minor source, or not a source.

The following analyses of financial, work, and residence variables are limited mainly to the first year in college. While it would be useful to know the effects of these contingencies after the first year, studies are difficult if the outcome variable is student attrition. Notice that once a student drops out of college, certain environmental experiences are precluded (living in a dormitory, work-study, scholarship support, and so forth). Even if the occurrence of such experiences subsequent to the freshman year has no causal relationship to attrition, there would be a built-in negative association between later occurrences and attrition simply because such experiences would be precluded once the student dropped out. Thus, such occurrences after the freshman year would be positively associated with persistence (and negatively associated with dropping out) because only persisters would be able to experience them. This problem of the possibility of artifactual effects after the freshman year will arise on several occasions later on in the chapter and in subsequent chapters.

In addition to the four financial aid items from the 1968 freshman questionnaire, a number of more detailed items were used from the follow-up questionnaire in 1972. The instructions for these questions read: "For each item below, indicate the extent to which it has been a source for financing your *undergraduate* education (include costs for both academic and living expenses)." Students were instructed to answer each item in terms of one of three alternatives—major source (50 percent or more), minor source, not a source. The items were: support from parents or relatives, support from spouse, fellowships or scholarships (federal, state, school or university, private foundation or organization, industry or business, other), loans (federal, state, commerical, other), withdrawals from savings or assets, GI benefits, ROTC benefits, and other sources.

Chapter Four treats employment in considerable detail, comparing work-study with other kinds of work. Here federally sponsored work-study programs are treated as financial aid. Sections below focus on the impact of six categories of financial aid: parental support, support from spouse, scholarships and grants, loans, work-study programs, and miscellaneous sources (GI bill, ROTC, savings, etc.). A concluding section will treat combinations of various aid sources known as financial aid "packages."

Parental Aid

Students rely on parental aid far more than any other single source. For nearly 65 percent of the white women, parental aid is a major source of support for their freshman undergraduate year, while only 16 percent receive no parental support. For 47 percent of the men, parental aid is a major source, while for only 28 percent it is not. Blacks are somewhat less likely than whites to rely on parental aid: only 33 percent depend on parental aid for major freshman support.

The expected[2] and actual dropout rates (in percentages) for white men and women are shown in Table 8, separately by degree of dependence on parental aid during the freshman year.

[2] Expected dropout rates were computed from four sets of predictors: student characteristics (Chapter Two), work status during the freshman year (Chapter Four), freshman residence (Chapter Five), and college characteristics (Chapter Six). These variables produced multiple correlations in the four samples as follows: white men (.443), white women (.418), blacks in black colleges (.440), and blacks in white colleges (.587).

Table 8.

DROPOUT RATES RELATED TO PARENTAL AID
(Percentages)

	Men		Women	
Extent of Parental Aid	Actual Dropout Rate	Expected Dropout Rate	Actual Dropout Rate	Expected Dropout Rate
Not a source	43	42	42	39
Minor source	40	39	32	31
Major source	32	33	28	29

Relying on parental support has a small but statistically significant positive effect on the student's ability to persist in college. For men, major parental support (versus no support) reduces dropout chances by about 2 percent. For women, the comparable reduction is about 4 percent. These figures illustrate dramatically the importance of controlling for differences in the student's initial propensity to drop out. Note that the difference in actual dropout rates for men favors those who depend on parental support as a major source by about 11 percent. For women, the comparable difference in actual dropout rates is still larger: about 14 percent. Without the accompanying expected dropout rates based on entering student characteristics and other environmental variables, one might conclude that the significance of parental support during the freshman year is much greater than it actually is. In other words, the differences in dropout rates among students with differing parental support for the freshman year can be attributed primarily to factors other than parental aid per se.

The actual and expected dropout rates for students with differing parental support were calculated separately for various types of colleges. The results are entirely consistent—small positive effect on persistence—for students in two- and four-year colleges, both public and private. Among students attending universities, however, particularly private universities, reliance on parental support appears to effect persistence *negatively*. This effect is especially pronounced among those students for whom parental aid is a minor source of freshman support. Compared with those who have no parental support, these students have dropout rates about 8 percent higher than expected. The high cost of attending a private university may be one explanation. Those who attend private universities may be handicapped in competition for financial aid if their parents provide some, but not all, of the support necessary to meet college expenses. Conceivably, students with no parental support find it easier to demonstrate the need that permits them to take full advantage of the financial aid available.

Additional analyses using level of parental *income* produced some interesting interaction effects. For women, the positive effect of parental aid was clear-cut among those in low-income (parental income below $10,000) and middle-income (between $10,000 and $20,000) brackets but *reversed* among high-income women (greater than $20,000). For men, on the other hand, the benefits of parental support were strongest within the high-income group (decreases of about 10 percent in dropout chances). One possible factor here is that high-income women who receive no parental aid are a highly select group (less than 4 percent of the no-aid category); high-income men whose parents provide no support are somewhat less special (about 7 percent of their group).

Does parental aid beyond the freshman year have an impact? An item similar to one on parental support on the freshman questionnaire was included in the 1972 follow-up. However, the follow-up item inquired about sources of support for the student's *entire* undergraduate education, rather than just the freshman year. As expected, the percentage of students who reported parental aid as a minor source is somewhat higher on the follow-up than on the freshman questionnaire, indicating that about 6 percent of the students who receive no support during the freshman year do receive some during subsequent years. The differences between expected and actual dropout rates based on the follow-up item are somewhat larger: about a 10 percent reduction in dropout rates for both men and women who receive parental aid compared with those who do not. The differences in impact between minor and major support are negligible. Continuing parental help beyond the freshman year appears to enhance the student's chances of finishing college.

For black students attending white colleges parental aid as major support is clearly associated with persistence. The decrease in dropout probabilities is 12 percent compared with those who have no support and 17 percent compared to those with only minor parental support. The comparable reductions for students attending black colleges are a negligible 1 percent. Parental support is not critical for students attending black colleges, but a major factor for black students attending white colleges. Without major parental support, these black students have substantially reduced chances of finishing.

Support from Spouse

Although married students constituted less than 2 percent of the entering student population in 1968, the effects of financial support from spouses are important. Of the men who are married when they start college, 55 percent have wives who provide financial support for college expenses, and four in five of these wives supply major support. Figures for women are even more striking. Seventy-one percent have husbands who help pay college expenses, and better than four in five of these husbands provide major rather than minor aid. Married persons—women in particular—who enter college depend heavily on their spouses for funds.

Because of the relatively small numbers of married black students, the analysis of spousal support will be confined to white students.[3] Expected and actual dropout rates for married students who receive spousal support contrast sharply. If the spouse provides major rather than no support, the reduction in a student's chances of dropping out is dramatic: 28 percent for men and 15 percent for women. However, if the spouse provides only minor support, the impact is *reversed:* dropout rates for men and women *increase* by 30 percent and 8 percent, respectively. While these findings are based on relatively small samples (approximately 50 married men and 50 married women reported minor financial support from their spouses), the dramatic contrast cannot be attributed to chance variations.

Why is the effect of minor spousal support apparently

[3] In several subsequent sections of the book, results for black students will not be reported whenever the sample size is too small.

negative? Such support may indicate that the spouse has an un-
certain employment situation. On a more subtle level, spouses who
are ambivalent or resentful about their partner's attending college
may provide only sporadic or little support. Whatever the explanation, providing only minor support may create uncertainties or
conflicts that militate against completing college. If nothing else,
married students might be well advised to reach a clear understanding about financial support from their spouses before they finalize
plans to enroll in college.

How does spousal support affect persistence among students
who get married after entering college? To explore this question, the
actual and estimated dropout rates were tabulated for the one student in six who married as an undergraduate. As expected, these
students rely less on their spouses for support than students who are
married when they enter college. While the percentage for the two
groups is the same—54 percent receive either major or minor
support—the majority (better than two in three) of those who
marry after entering college receive only minor support from their
spouses. Similarly, among the 60 percent of women who rely on
their husbands for support, nearly two in three receive only minor
support. Apparently, most students who marry in college continue
to rely on other sources, only infrequently shifting to the spouse as
a major source.

Both groups substantially improve their chances of finishing
college if they are able to rely on their spouses for financial support. Compared with students whose spouses are not a source of
support, those with major support have a much better chance of
finishing college: a 15 percent and 18 percent increase, respectively,
for men and women. Even minor (compared with no) support is
beneficial: a 14 percent and 20 percent increase, respectively, for
men and women. Clearly, the unwillingness or inability of the
spouse to provide financial support, no matter how substantial, is a
negative prognostic sign for college students who contemplate
marriage before completing their undergraduate work.

Scholarships and Grants

Although scholarships and grants are the most coveted
forms of financial aid, only about a third of the white students (31
percent of the men and 36 percent of the women) receive this

support for their freshman expenses. About equal numbers receive major and minor support. Scholarships and grants are much more frequent sources for black students: among blacks attending black colleges and those enrolled in white colleges, 54 percent and 53 percent, respectively, receive scholarships or grants during their freshman year.

Scholarships give the recipient only a slight advantage over the nonrecipient in persistence. These positive effects are small for men (3 percent reduction in dropout probabilities) and negligible for women (less than 1 percent). Once again, these results strongly justify the use of expected dropout rates in making analyses: compared with students who have no scholarships, those with major support have substantially higher dropout rates: 12 percent and 9 percent, respectively, for men and women. Differences in the expected dropout rates, however, are almost as large: 9 percent and 8 percent, respectively. In short, the observed differences in dropout rates among students receiving differing amounts of scholarship support can be attributed largely to factors other than the scholarship.

Analyses of the effects of scholarship or grant aid in relation to the income level of the students' parents again produced some interesting interactions. Among the men, the positive impact of scholarships and grants was clear-cut on those from middle-income families: about 3 percent reduction in dropout chances associated with minor grant support and 5 percent with major support. Among the women, the positive effects appeared to be confined to those in the low-income group. Among men in the high-income group (parental income above $20,000) major grant support was associated with a reduction in dropout rates of 9 percent, but minor support was accompanied by an *increase* of 10 percent.

Do these borderline results apply to all forms of scholarship support, or are differences associated with a particular type of grant? The follow-up provides opportunity to estimate the impact of six different types of scholarship support. However, a word of caution is in order. Since the students responded to the questionnaire in terms of their entire undergraduate education, some students may not have received their initial scholarships until after the freshman year. Among those who begin college without any scholarship aid, students who drop out early lose any chance they might have had for later receiving a scholarship. Those who stay in college, on the other hand, remain eligible for such aid as they remain studious. Under these circumstances, a correlation between dropping out and specific forms of financial aid could be simply an artifact of differences in opportunity between dropouts and persisters, rather than the result of a causal relationship between scholarship aid and persistence. In short, data from the follow-up which suggest a negative effect of any form of aid on persistence should be regarded as strong evidence of a causal relationship, whereas data suggesting a positive impact must be viewed with considerable caution.

By far the most common sources of scholarships and grants are state governments and institutions. Although about one in six men and women receive support from these sources, for about two-thirds of the recipients these are minor rather than major sources. Both forms of scholarships are associated with student persistence. As with freshman scholarship support, the impact appears somewhat greater for men: the average reduction in dropout probabilities associated with these scholarships is 8 percent and 4 percent, respectively, for men and women. Again, these results should be interpreted with caution, particularly for institutional scholarships, which are frequently awarded after the freshman year.

Nine percent of both sexes receive Educational Opportunity Grants from the federal government. However, 54 percent of the men receive major support from their federal grants, compared with only 32 percent of the women. This discrepancy is consistent with the finding that men receive substantially larger scholarship stipends than women (Astin and Christian, 1975).

To relate federal grants and attrition: men who receive minor support from these grants show a moderate reduction in dropout chances (7 percent) compared with men who do not have grants, but men who receive major support from their federal grants show no such advantage. Among the women, federal grants (both major and minor) are associated with a 5 percent reduction in dropout probabilities. Again, these findings must be viewed with caution, since students who do not receive federal Educational Opportunity Grants during their freshman year are still eligible in subsequent years, if they remain in college.

Approximately 6 percent of the men and 9 percent of the women receive private foundation grants while in college. These are apparently much smaller than grants from public and institutional sources, since for about 80 percent of the recipients they provide only minor support. Data on expected and actual dropout rates provide a consistent picture: receiving foundation grants is associated with modest reductions in dropout probabilities (4 percent for men and 6 percent for women). Since most foundation scholarships are probably awarded at the time the student enters college (for example, the National Merit Scholarships), a spurious effect seems less likely here than with institutional, state, and federal grants.

Scholarships from business or industry support 4 percent of the men and 2 percent of the women. Compared with other scholarship support, a scholarship from a business or industrial firm is *negatively* associated with college persistence. Thus, compared with students who do not have such scholarships, those who receive major support from business or industry have increased dropout probabilities of 12 percent (men) and 6 percent (women). Why these scholarships should be negatively associated with college persistence is unclear. Recipients may sometimes leave college to go to work for the sponsoring firm, or they may attend specialized institutions with poor holding power. The conditions of such scholarships may involve alternate periods of full-time undergraduate study and employment with the sponsoring business or industry. This latter explanation may be deficient since similar results are obtained when the analysis is repeated with a more stringent definition of dropping out (that is, when stopouts are included among persisters). If students are merely stopping out for periods of work, including the stopouts among the persisters rather than among the dropouts should reduce this apparently negative effect. On the other hand, working at jobs as part of an academic program seems to be related to dropping out (see Chapter Four).

The final source of scholarship aid is a catch-all category: "other scholarships, fellowships." Since only about 5 percent of the students receive support in this category, the other categories appear to cover most major sources of scholarship or grant assistance. Results here are mixed. Men with major or minor support and women with minor support have a decreased dropout probability of about 7 percent. Women with major support (less than one in five) have an *increased* dropout probability of about 10 percent. Such anomalous results defy explanation, although they do suggest that the *amount* of scholarship support from private sources bears substantially on the student's chances of finishing college. However, since scholarships in this category are an unknown quantity (many could have been awarded after the freshman year), the results should be treated with caution.

Expected dropout rates provide insights into how scholarship or grant aid is awarded. On the one hand, if scholarships are awarded on merit, the expected dropout rates of scholarship recipients should be low (that is, the more academically able student has a relatively small chance of dropping out). On the other hand, if scholarships are awarded for need, the recipients should have higher expected dropout rates (or, at a minimum, rates not appreciably different from those of nonrecipients). Overall, merit appears to be a more important criterion than financial need: expected dropout rates of freshman recipients are about 10 percent lower than those of nonrecipients. Expected rates for those whose scholarships are a major support source are not appreciably different from those whose scholarships provide only minor support. This pattern changes somewhat, however, when the data for scholarship aid as reported on the 1972 follow-up are examined. Here the expected dropout rates are lowest among the students for whom scholarships are a *minor* source of support. Students with no scholarship support have expected dropout rates roughly equal to those of students whose scholarships are a major support source.

These findings are probably due to several factors. First, the lower expected dropout rates of scholarship recipients as a group suggest that scholarships are awarded in part on merit. Second, the higher expected dropout rates among major compared with minor recipients reflect the greater dropout propensity of students whose financial need is sufficient to qualify them for larger awards. In other words, students with greater financial need are probably more dropout-prone to begin with. Finally, the lower expected dropout rates among students with minor scholarship support may be evidence of the artifact above: the longer students stay in college, the greater the probability that they will be able to avail themselves of scholarship aid. If such aid is secured late in the student's undergraduate career, it counts for only a minor portion of college costs. If this explanation is valid, it underscores the necessity to interpret any results based on the follow-up with caution.

Analyses of scholarship support and persistence among black students also produce somewhat inconsistent findings. In the black colleges, students with major grant support have a somewhat reduced (4 percent) chance of dropping out. Receiving minor grant support, however, is associated with a 5 percent *increase* in dropout chances. For blacks attending white colleges, the situation is reversed: minor grant support is associated with an 8 percent decrease in dropout probabilities, while major support is associated with a small increase in dropout chances (1 percent). This latter finding confirms the recent study by Baber and Caple (1970), which showed a facilitative effect of scholarships among blacks attending a predominantly white university in the Midwest. While these data on blacks are difficult to rationalize, they suggest that the *amount* of scholarship aid may be critical to the black student's chances of completing college.

Loans

From the standpoint of public policy, loans represent one of the most controversial sources of financial aid. Proponents of loan programs are attracted by the relatively low cost, arguing that limited resources can be made available to many more students if they are heavily concentrated in loan programs. Some critics object to burdening students with long-term debts, while others point to allegedly high default rates.

Two recent studies have produced equivocal results on the effects of loans. Blanchfield (1971) reports that the percentage of costs financed by loan support is not related to persistence. Trent and Medsker (1967) find that students who *seek* loans are more likely to stay in college; their findings, however, are subject to the artifact already described (that is, the longer a student stays in college, the greater his or her chances to seek a loan).

Students entering college in 1968 relied somewhat less on loans than on scholarships or grants. Less than one student in four (21 percent of the men and 24 percent of the women) received loans to support their college expenses during the freshman year. For approximately three recipients in five, loans constitute a major source of support.

For men, depending on loan support during the freshman year has a consistently negative effect on persistence. On the average, reliance on loan support increases a man's chances of dropping out by about 6 percent. This effect occurs, regardless of whether the support is major or minor, in all types of institutions. (It is pronounced in the private two-year colleges, where reliance on loans appears to increase male dropout rates by about 15 percent.) The effect is especially clear-cut among men at low- and middle-income levels; results for men at the highest level (parental income over $20,000) are indefinite because of the small number.

The picture for women is less consistent. In general, women who rely on loans as a major source of support compared with women who have no loan support have slightly increased chances of dropping out (about 2 percent), particularly if their parents are in the middle-income bracket ($10,000-20,000). Reliance on loans as a minor source, however, appears to have a *positive* impact on persistence (6 percent reduction in dropout rates) for women attending public institutions (whether universities or four- or two-year colleges). Reliance on loans as a minor source has a slight negative effect on persistence among women at private institutions. Assuming that minor support at a private institution involves larger amounts than at a public institution, it appears that the amount of the loan is critical to the persistence rates of women. Small loans appear to benefit undergraduate women, but larger loans seem to present a handicap to completing college. Men, on the other hand, appear handicapped by loans, regardless of size.

The picture for the impact of loans on black students is also somewhat unclear. While loans have no consistent effect on persistence among blacks attending black colleges, they appear to be an asset for black students at white colleges. For this latter group, reliance on loans as either a major or minor source of support for the freshman year is associated with an 8 percent reduction in drop-out rates.

The loan items from the four-year follow-up questionnaire indicate that the highest proportion of students (20 percent) rely on federal loans, followed by state (9 percent), commercial (9 percent)', and "other" loans (4 percent). The relationship of these items to attrition is not consistent with the above results for loans during the freshman year. Loans (and particularly state loans) tend to be positively associated with persistence, especially among women. In all likelihood, this association is not causal, but rather an artifact. Thus, the longer a student is able to remain in college, the greater the opportunity to secure a loan. That students were much more likely to report loans as a minor source of support on the follow-up than on the freshman questionnaire supports this interpretation.

To speculate on the negative impact of loans on persistence among men: since estimates of dropout probabilities control for differences in financial need, such as family income and concern about college finances, one might expect men who secure loans to have an easier time getting through college simply because they have additional resources. But precisely the opposite occurs. Apparently, any short-term financial advantage associated with securing a loan is outweighed by other, possibly psychological factors. Do men who begin college dependent on loans quickly become disenchanted with the prospect of long-term indebtedness, once indebtedness from the first year becomes a reality? For some men, leaving college may be a more desirable alternative than incurring further indebtedness. Whatever the reasons, the psychological and motivational aspects of loans and indebtedness merit careful consideration in the development of future financial aid policy.

Work-Study Programs

Although work-study programs are a form of work, certain work-study findings are presented here because these programs have been a major part of federal financial aid policy since the Higher Education Act of 1965.

During their freshman year (1968–1969), 3 percent of the

men and and 6 percent of the women participated in federally sponsored work-study programs. By the time of the four-year follow-up in 1972, 9 percent of the men and 13 percent of the women had participated. For more than 75 percent of these students, work-study provides only minor support for their college expenses.

Analyses of expected and actual dropout rates indicate that participation in work-study programs during the freshman year results in a small but significant increase in student persistence (2 percent and 6 percent reduction in dropout rates for men and women, respectively). The follow-up suggests that participation in work-study at any time during the undergraduate years is associated with somewhat larger reductions in dropout rates: 8 percent for men and 11 percent for women. (The significance of these larger rates is, of course, open to some question because of the artifacts discussed above.)

Data by parental income level suggest that federal work-study programs are most likely to have positive effects on students at middle-income ($10,000-20,000) levels. The impact of work-study among black students is much more striking. Not only are blacks more apt to participate in work-study programs during the freshman year (11 percent from black colleges and 12 percent from white colleges), but participation is associated with a more substantial reduction in dropout rates: 14 percent in black colleges and 9 percent in white colleges.

Work-study programs are an attractive form of financial aid. Such programs not only offer productive work, but also increase the student's chances of completing college. These positive effects might be attributable to the greater degree of student involvement in campus life that may result from participation in work-study programs (see Chapters Four and Five).

Other Forms

One financial aid item from the freshman questionnaire, "personal savings and/or employment," covers a number of sources, including money earned by the student from earlier employment, inheritances, work-study, and other employment. Seventy-four percent of the white men and 63 percent of the white women finance their freshman year in part by such funds. For about half the men utilizing this source, the funds provide major support, whereas they constitute a major source for less than one-third of the women. Fewer blacks depend on such funds as either a major or minor source: 53 percent in white colleges and 38 percent in black colleges.

Again, analysis of expected and actual dropout rates produces a mixed picture. For white women, the effects of dependence on this source during the freshman year are generally negative, associated with increased dropout rates of about 2 percent. These negative effects are much more pronounced for women attending public and private two-year colleges, where the average increase was about 6 percent. In direct contrast, white men at two-year colleges who rely on this source during the freshman year have an average *decrease* in dropout probabilities of about 5 percent. Men at public four-year colleges and universities *increase* their chances of dropping out by about 4 percent. Although it is difficult to explain these discrepancies, that this category includes support from many sources may account in part for the varied results.

Further clues to the possible impact of reliance on savings are provided in the follow-up questionnaire, which contains an item mentioning savings, "withdrawals from savings, assets," as distinct from employment or other aid sources. Both men and women rely heavily on this specific support (39 percent and 35 percent, respectively). For about one-fourth of those, these funds provide major support for undergraduate expenses. Reliance is associated with *increased* dropout rates among both men (7 percent) and women (4 percent). Reliance on savings as a minor source, by contrast, is associated with decreased dropout rates (3 percent for men and 4 percent for women). Among blacks, reliance on savings or assets as a major source of support also has a pronounced negative effect on persistence at white colleges (an increase in dropout probabilities of 29 percent). No effect is observed among blacks at black colleges.

Several factors may explain these findings. On the one hand, the positive association with minor reliance on savings or assets may result from the artifact: the longer a person remains in college, the more possibilities arise that may require savings or other assets to support college and living expenses. On the other hand, the negative association between major reliance and persistence must be regarded as strong evidence of causal relationship. In all likelihood, entering college students who have substantial liquid resources (savings, trust funds, and so on) are ineligible for the usual forms of financial aid. Forced to utilize their assets for substantial support, these students may ultimately view college as unreasonably expensive and see dropping out as a way to conserve assets. Whatever the explanation, these data should be considered in any future attempts to revise standard procedures for defining financial need.

About 6 percent of the men and 1 percent of the women rely on GI benefits to support their undergraduate costs. For three-fourths of these men, GI benefits provide major support for their college costs, while the same is true for only 60 percent of the women. (This discrepancy probably reflects the failure to distinguish between student benefits from their own military service and *from their parents' service;* presumably, a larger proportion of the women are reporting support from their parents.) Among the white men, reliance on GI benefits is negatively associated with persistence: college men who rely on GI funds for major support have an increased dropout probability of about 7 percent. Among women minor reliance is associated with increased dropout chances and major reliance with slightly decreased dropout chances; however, the small samples make these findings highly tentative. Too few blacks at black colleges received GI-bill support to derive any estimates of its effects, but among blacks at white colleges, the impact is negative: 8 percent increase in dropout probabilities.

Why reliance on the GI bill should be associated with dropping out is not entirely clear. Since virtually all veterans entering college in 1968 were eligible for some GI support, veteran status, in effect, has been confounded with GI support. Possibly, the effects of being a veteran are showing up rather than the effects of GI support per se. That the GI group is atypical to begin with is reflected in the expected dropout rates: 58 percent for men receiving major GI support versus 35 percent for those receiving none (the comparable percentages for women are 41 percent and 31 percent). For blacks at white colleges, the corresponding expected dropout rates are 70 percent and 48 percent, respectively, for GI recipients and nonrecipients. It may well be that veterans (many from the Vietnam war) find it exceedingly difficult to adjust to traditional college life.

A final category of financial aid support is ROTC benefits. About 2 percent of the white men and virtually no white women receive ROTC benefits. For more than 80 percent of the recipients, this aid constitutes major support. Men whose ROTC benefits are a major source of support for undergraduate expenses have a substantially reduced dropout rate (14 percent) compared with students who do not receive ROTC benefits. (Data for blacks are too sparse for reliable estimates.) Participation in ROTC may represent a commitment that greatly decreases the chances that the student will leave college. Among other things, ROTC is contractual: students who receive benefits normally make a commitment to continue in the program and to serve on active duty once they finish college. Whatever the explanation, ROTC programs are "cost effective" in the sense that they are associated with substantially increased probabilities of degree completion. Indeed, even though the expected dropout chances of students receiving major support from ROTC are low to begin with (only 24 percent compared with 37 percent for non-ROTC students), their actual dropout rate is much lower (only 9 percent). Thus, of those students who receive ROTC benefits while in college (whether major or minor), fewer than one in ten fails to finish college.

Packages

The financial aid provisions of the Higher Education Act of 1965 authorize institutions to use financial aid "packages" that combine three basic sources of support: grants, loans, and work-study programs. So far these three forms of aid have been considered separately in terms of their relationship to student persistence. Combinations of these three may also have an impact on persistence. Since dealing with combinations reduces the number of students in each category, only the results for white students are presented here.

Grants and Loans. Receipt of these two forms of aid tends to be correlated. Thus, among students who receive no grant support, only 17 percent receive any loan support. By contrast, 35 percent of those who receive either minor or major grant support also receive loan support. Among those who receive no loan support, only 28 percent receive any scholarship support, compared with 52 percent among those who receive either minor or major loan support. Approximately 2 percent of the men and 4 percent of the women receive major support from both sources. However, among students from the low-income bracket (less than $10,000), the percentages are higher: 8 percent of the men and 12 percent of the women.

The positive effect of grants on persistence is most obvious among men with no loan support and virtually nonexistent among students with major loan support. Dependence on loans, on the one hand, impairs the normally positive effect of scholarships. The negative effect of loans on persistence, on the other hand, is consistent among all groups of men, regardless of their status in terms of grant support. However, this negative effect is most pronounced among men who receive minor grant support (about 5 percent increase in dropout chances compared with men who receive major support or no support from grants).

No clear-cut interactions between grant and loan support are apparent among the women. Receiving minor loan support has a modest positive effect on persistence (about 3 percent), regardless of the women's grant status. Similarly, grants have negligible effects on persistence regardless of the women's loan status.

Grants and Work-Study. Receipt of grant support is positively associated with participation in federal work-study programs. Only 1 percent of men with no grants participate in work-study programs, compared with 5 percent of those who receive major grant support. The association is even stronger among the women, where only 3 percent of those with no grants participate in work-study, compared with 13 percent of those who receive major grant support.

The effects on persistence of participation in work-study seem to depend on the student's grant status. The most clear-cut positive effect occurs among students receiving no grants: decreases in dropout probabilities of 4 percent and 11 percent respectively, for men and women. The comparable figures for students receiving major grant support are only 1 percent and 5 percent, whereas the effects of work-study are actually *negative* among those receiving minor grant support: an increase in dropout probabilities of 6 percent for both sexes.

The effects of grant support also appear to depend on students' work-study status. For men and women, any benefits from grant support disappear among students participating in work-study. For men in work-study, major grant support versus no grant has no effect on dropout probabilities, whereas receiving minor support is associated with a 9 percent *increase* in dropout probabilities. This interaction between grants and work-study is even more dramatic among women. Thus, even though grants have no consistent overall effect, among women on work-study programs major grant support is associated with a 6 percent increase and minor grant support with a 15 percent increase in dropout probabilities.

Thus, grants in combination with work-study may not make effective financial aid packages. In particular, work-study and minor grant support may represent an unwise combination of financial assistance.

Loans and Work-Study. Participation in work-study programs is positively associated with dependence on loan support. Only 1 percent of the men who receive no loan support during their freshman year participate in work-study programs, compared with 6 percent of those who receive major loan support. The corresponding percentages for women are 3 percent and 11 percent.

The effects of participation in work-study appear to depend heavily on the student's loan status. For the student receiving major loan support, participation reduces the chances of dropping out (13 percent for men and 5 percent for women). However, participation appears to have a negative effect on persistence (10 percent *increase* in dropout rates for both men and women) if the student receives only minor loan support.

Grants, Loans, and Work-Study. Receiving all three forms of financial aid is closely associated with the income level of the students' parents. Among the low-income students, 1.3 percent of the men and 3.8 percent of the women received some support from grants, loans, and work-study programs during the freshman year.

Comparable percentages among middle-income students were 0.3 and 1.0, respectively, for men and women; among high-income students, less than one-tenth of 1 percent received support from all three sources.

Because of the small numbers of students involved, it is possible to examine the simultaneous impact of these three sources of aid only among students from low-income families. Receiving support from federal work-study programs seems to enhance persistence maximally (8 percent for men and 18 percent for women) when the low-income student has *neither* grant nor loan support during the freshman year. On the other hand, work-study is associated with increased dropout rates (6 percent for men and 10 percent for women) if the low-income student has major grant support coupled with minor loan support. However, work-study and major loan support have positive effects on persistence, regardless of the degree of grant support (if any).

The particular types of financial aid which make up any student's package may be important to the ability to complete college. While the complexities and ambiguities of this study underscore the need for more in-depth research on the impact of particular packages, certain preliminary generalizations seem warranted. First, grants in combinations with loans do not make particularly effective financial aid packages. In particular, a combination containing small amounts of grant and loan support seems unwise. Second, mixing work-study programs with minor grant or loan support is also not recommended. Third, the most effective combination appears to be substantial loan support and work-study.

Summary

The evidence presented in this chapter indicates that the source and amount of financial aid can be an important factor in the student's ability to complete college. Although many of the findings must be regarded as tentative because of limitations in the data, several general conclusions seem warranted.

1. Receiving support from parents for college expenses generally enhances the student's ability to complete college. This facilitative effect occurs among students in all income groups, except

women who come from high-income brackets. For them, receiving parental support appears to contribute negatively to college persistence.

2. Students who are married when they enter college persist better if their spouses provide major support for their college costs. If the spouse is able only to provide minor help, however, the effect is reversed, and the student is better off having no support. Among students who marry after entering college, assistance from the spouse facilitates persistence, regardless of the amount.

3. Scholarships or grants are associated with small increases in student persistence rates. These beneficial effects are confined largely to women from low-income families and to men from middle income families. The amount of the grant support appears to be a major factor in student persistence, particularly among black students.

4. Reliance on loans is associated with decreased persistence among men in all income groups. Among women, the effects are highly variable, depending on the amount of the loan support and the income level of the woman's parents. Reliance on loans is associated with increased persistence among black students attending white colleges.

5. Participation in federal work-study programs seems to enhance student persistence, particularly among women and blacks. Work-study has its most consistent positive impact among students from middle-income families.

6. Reliance on savings or other assets appears to decrease the student's chances of finishing college. This effect was observed among both men and women, and among blacks attending white colleges.

7. Reliance on GI-bill support is negatively associated with student persistence, although the confounding of such support with being a veteran makes it difficult to determine whether this type of aid, as such, is related to persistence.

8. Support from ROTC stipends is strongly associated with increased student persistence.

9. Given the finite amount of aid available in most federal, state, and institutional programs, administrators and policy-makers are often confronted with choices about how these limited resources

should be allocated among various types of support. Results of the current study suggest that student persistence will be maximized if funds are concentrated in work-study programs and, to a lesser extent, in grant programs rather than in loans. For men, the advantages of grant support and work-study support versus loans are roughly equivalent: Dropout chances are about 8 percent less. For women, work-study versus loans (8 percent reduction in dropout chances) is clearly superior to grants versus loans (3 percent reduction).

10. Analyses of various financial aid packages (involving combinations of grants, loans, and work-study) produced a number of findings that may have important policy implications. In general, any form of aid appears to be most effective if it is *not* combined with other forms. This is particularly true in the case of work-study programs, which tend to lose their beneficial impact when combined with grants or loans. This loss of impact is especially marked among low-income students. Similarly, grants are most effective if the student has no loan. The only combination which is associated with greater persistence is work-study and major (rather than minor) loan support. These tentative findings underscore the need for more in-depth studies of the impact of various financial aid packages. Such studies should examine not only various packages, but also possible interactions of these packages with the student's race and sex and with parental income.

4

EFFECTS OF
EMPLOYMENT

The relationship between student employment and persistence in college raises a number of policy issues for institutional administrators and policy-makers. What kinds of jobs should be made available for students? Does employment interfere with the student's ability to finish college? How important is the number of hours worked? Should the work experience be integrated with the academic program? Does it matter whether the work takes place on campus or off campus? To plan and fund effective work and placement programs, institutional administrators and policy-makers need answers to these questions.

Since the decision to work or not to work may often be made independent of any institutional programs, students can also utilize information bearing on such questions. Should the student limit the number of hours worked? Should the job be on campus or off campus? Does marital status make any difference?

To explore the relationship between student persistence and various conditions of employment, information on employment status was obtained from two sets of items on the 1972 follow-up questionnaire. In the first set, students indicated their employment status *while enrolled during the freshman year.* The four options, together with the percentages of students who checked each, are shown in Table 9.

Table 9.

TYPES OF WORK BY FRESHMEN
(Percentages)

Types of Employment	White Men	White Women	Blacks in Black Colleges	Blacks in White Colleges
Federally sponsored work-study programs	2.4	5.2	11.1	11.9
Other on-campus work	6.3	8.6	4.4	5.9
Off-campus work	21.9	15.1	7.5	13.8
Employment for college credit as part of departmental program	2.1	.4	.2	.7

These data reveal some notable differences between blacks and whites. For example, the majority of whites working on campus are employed in programs other than federal work-study. For blacks, the situation is reversed: most are in federal work-study programs. Clearly, work-study provided the bulk of the employment for black students on both black and white college campuses. Another racial difference is evident among off-campus workers: only about half as many black freshmen attending black colleges have off-campus jobs as white freshmen or blacks attending white colleges. Perhaps black colleges are less effective in finding off-campus jobs; possibly their predominantly rural location or their concentration in the southern or border states may limit available off-campus employment opportunities.

The second set of items concerns the job the student held longest while in college. Students were asked how many hours per week they worked, how well the job fit their long-range career plans, how much they liked or disliked the work, and whether the work was beneficial or detrimental to their continuing in college. The five job categories, with the percentages of students who checked each, are shown in Table 10. More than two-thirds of all students

Table 10.
TYPES OF JOBS HELD LONGEST WHILE IN COLLEGE
(Percentages)

Longest Job	White Men	White Women	Blacks in Black Colleges	Blacks in White Colleges
Teaching or research assistant to a professor	3.6	3.8	3.9	3.5
Work in some other academic-related department on campus (such as library, administration)	5.4	13.1	18.8	16.3
Work in nonacademic sector of the campus (for example, cafeteria, dorm)	11.3	13.7	14.7	10.7
Work off campus in area related to course work	11.0	7.4	7.6	12.4
Work off campus in area *not* related to course work	39.4	27.7	17.4	33.5

are employed at some time while enrolled in college. Blacks attending white colleges show the highest degree of employment (76 percent), whereas blacks attending black colleges show the lowest rate (62 percent). The percentages for different types of work generally correspond to those reported earlier for the freshman year: with the exception of blacks attending black colleges, students are much more likely to be employed off than on campus. As a matter of fact, the low rate of off-campus employment for blacks in black colleges

(about half that of other groups) accounts for the difference between the employment rates of blacks attending black colleges and
rates for other groups of black and white students.

The effects of work on persistence will be examined from
several different perspectives: type of work, number of hours, relevance of work to career, job satisfaction, marital status, and financial aid.

Type of Work

Jobs may be classified by their physical location (on campus
versus off campus) and their relationship to the student's academic
program. Unless indicated otherwise, "dropouts" here include both
dropouts and stopouts.

On Campus. Although participation in federal work-study
programs is associated with student persistence (see Chapter Three),
additional data on expected[1] and actual dropout rates for students
with other on-campus employment during the freshman year suggest that such work also has a positive impact. Participation for white
men and women is associated with a modest (4 percent) reduction
in dropout probabilities, whereas involvement of blacks attending
white colleges is associated with a 13 percent reduction. There is
no significant association for blacks at black colleges. Apparently,
having a campus job during the freshman year strongly increases
the student's chances of finishing college.

Does the impact of on-campus employment depend on the
type of work? Apparently not. Both work in an academic-related
department and work in a non-academic part of the campus have
similar positive effects for men and women and for blacks and whites.
Indeed, the effects of the job held longest while the student was
in college are more striking than those of the job held during the
freshman year. Among white students, a 9 percent reduction in
dropout probabilities for both men and women is associated with

---

[1] Expected dropout rates were computed from freshman student data,
as well as data on financial aid during the freshman year, freshman residence,
and college characteristics. Multiple correlations using these variables for the
four groups are: white men (.438), white women (.416), blacks in black
colleges (.425), and blacks in white colleges (.583).

working longest at a job in either an academic or nonacademic sector. Black students attending white colleges who hold such jobs show a 20 percent reduction in dropout probabilities, while blacks in black colleges show a 15 percent reduction if the job they held longest is academic and a 6 percent reduction if it is nonacademic.

Several factors may account for the positive effects of on-campus employment. One is simply economic: students who have jobs are more financially secure to continue their studies than students with comparable financial backgrounds who are unable to get jobs. Another factor may be psychological. A regular job on the college campus necessarily means that the student will be spending more time on campus and interacting more with fellow students and staff. For many students, greater involvement in campus life and activities may help to develop a stronger sense of identification with the institution which serves as a deterrent to dropping out. This involvement is strongly reinforced by other findings below and in subsequent chapters.

Off Campus. On the surface, findings for off-campus employment seem inconsistent. On one hand, working at an off-campus job *during the freshman year* is associated with persistence among both men and women (8 percent and 5 percent decrease in dropout probabilities, respectively), and among blacks in white colleges (5 percent reduction). An off-campus job as the job held longest during the undergraduate years, on the other hand, is negatively associated with persistence in all four student samples. On the average, being employed longest in an off-campus job is associated with increased dropout probabilities of approximately 5 percent among blacks and whites. However, when those students who work off campus during the freshman year are omitted, off-campus work as the job held longest is associated with a much larger increase in dropout chances (about 15 percent). Apparently, students who do not hold off-campus jobs during the freshman year but later obtain them encounter special difficulties that interfere with completing college. This apparent reversal of impact, noted below, is attributable almost entirely to the greater number of hours worked by those who obtain jobs off campus after the freshman year.

The potential problems associated with off-campus employment are further highlighted by the students' responses to the question, "Indicate whether holding a job while enrolled in college was beneficial, detrimental, or made no difference to continuing in college." While most students (89 percent of the men and 94 percent of the women) felt that their jobs were either beneficial or made no difference, the largest percentages reporting that their jobs were detrimental held off-campus jobs.

Employment for College Credit. Employment for credit as part of a departmental program during the freshman year is associated with an increased chance of dropping out: 5 percent for white men and 4 percent for white women. Results for blacks are based on too few cases to be reliable. Although, at first glance, these findings also defy explanation, it turns out (see below) that the impact of such employment is negative because it typically involves off-campus employment with long hours.

Number of Hours

The number of hours worked while the student attended college was assessed in terms of six categories: less than 5, 5–9, 10–14, 15–19, 20–24, and 25 or more hours per week. For simplicity, this last category was considered full-time work.

The number of hours is closely associated with the type of work performed. Students who hold work-study appointments or other on-campus jobs typically work between 15 and 19 hours per week. Students with off-campus jobs tend to put in somewhat longer hours—20 or more per week. Men tend to work longer hours than women: 36 percent of the men and 23 percent of the women in work-study programs work 20 hours or more per week. Among those in other on-campus jobs, 40 percent of the men and 23 percent of the women work 20 or more hours. Among those with off-campus jobs, two-thirds of the men but only half the women work 20 or more hours.

Working full-time has a consistently negative effect on persistence within all four groups. The differences are considerable: working full-time rather than, say, 15 to 19 hours per week is associated with a 15 percent increase in dropout rates among women and a 13 percent increase among men. Comparable differences exist within both samples of black students. These findings are consistent with those of Cohen, Brawer, and Connor (1969), and Kosher and Bellamy (1969), who report a negative relationship between persistence and the number of hours per week that students are employed.

The impact of full-time work depends somewhat on the type of work and the sex of the student. Working full-time at an off-campus job has a uniformly negative impact, regardless of whether the work is related to the student's course of study. If the off-campus job is unrelated to the course work, however, the negative impact of full-time employment is greater for the women (about 15 percent increase in dropout probabilities). As a matter of fact, this negative effect begins to appear when a women works more than 19 hours per week. Thus, for women working off-campus in unrelated jobs, 20 or more hours per week constitutes the equivalent of full-time work.

The negative effects of full-time employment also appear if the woman is employed in a job on campus, but no such effects appear among men employed in full-time campus jobs. Apparently, college men are better able than college women to tolerate full-time work, particularly if the employment is on campus.

Conceivably, men tend to get campus jobs that permit them to work large numbers of hours at times that are unlikely to interfere with academic work (evenings, weekends, etc.). If women who work relatively long hours are employed in clerical jobs, they probably have less flexible hours and are more likely to be forced to work between 9 and 5.

These apparently contradictory findings on off-campus employment are better understood in the light of the number of hours worked and the sequence of off-campus employment from the freshman through subsequent years. One reason why off-campus employment during the freshman year has a more favorable effect on student persistence than such employment in subsequent years is that students who work off campus as freshmen are likely to work fewer hours. A more important reason for the discrepancy, however, is the sequence of employment. If a student works at a part-time job off campus during the freshman year and continues in subsequent years, the impact of this pattern on persistence is generally positive: a reduction in dropout chances of about 8 percent for men and 6 percent for women. However, if the off-campus employment is initiated after the freshman year, the positive effect for women disappears and the effect for men actually becomes negative (about a 4 percent increase in dropout rate).

Apparently, the continuity of the student's employment status is important in off-campus work. If the student establishes a pattern of off-campus employment early, the effects tend to be positive as long as the number of hours is kept under control. If the student obtains an off-campus job after being unemployed or employed on campus during the freshman year, the impact tends to be negative. This reversal may simply mean that the student has encountered unforeseen financial difficulties.

Clearly, the beneficial effects of work noted earlier may be lost entirely if the student is forced to work full-time. For those students who work only a modest number of hours (say, fewer than twenty per week), the positive impact of employment is substantially greater than that reported previously: about a 10 percent decrease in dropout probabilities for men and women and for blacks and whites.

The reasons that full-time work might decrease the student's chances of completing college are numerous. Working full time does, of course, leave the student less time for study, but then part-time work *facilitates* student persistence (that is, it is an improvement over no work at all). Students can, apparently, tolerate a substantial investment of time in work without suffering any untoward effects on their academic progress.

Another, more subtle explanation concerns involvement. A campus job that requires a modest portion of the student's time may involve that student in campus activities to a greater extent than if the student had no campus job. However, a full-time job, particularly if it involves activities that separate the student from the mainstream of campus life, may be a significant distraction from studies and social life. That women who work on campus are positively affected by part-time work and negatively affected by full-time work may reflect differences in the types of jobs. The typical part-time job (in the bookstore, cafeteria, dormitory, or library, for instance) may bring the student frequently into contact with other students and faculty. Many full-time jobs, however, may be clerical (such as in the finance office or departmental offices) and involve fewer contacts with students and faculty. Such jobs also tend to have less flexible working hours.

Still another explanation for the negative effects of full-time and off-campus work concerns financial need. Students who work full time may be in a highly tenuous financial situation. Financial problems would be especially frequent among students who started college without an off-campus job but who subsequently obtained one. For such students, full-time work may be as much a symptom of dropout-proneness as it is a cause. Note that dropout-proneness, as reflected in estimates of dropout probabilities, is positively associated with the number of hours worked. Students employed full time, in other words, show greater dropout-proneness at college entrance than students who work part time.

In summary, the effects of the number of hours worked suggest that policy-makers and administrators can reduce student dropout rates by providing greater opportunities for part-time employment, especially on campus. Student requests for full-time work should probably be regarded as symptoms of possible financial problems or other difficulties that may eventually lead to dropping out. If the student's desire for full-time work is based on financial need, administrators might be well advised to seek other financial support to obviate the need for full-time work.

Relevance of Work to Career

The follow-up questionnaire asked a number of questions about the job held longest by the student while in college. Students were asked, "How well did your job during college fit in with your long-range career plans?" Students could pick one of five responses: "very well," "fairly well," "hardly at all," "not at all," "I have no long-range career plans." Only 6 percent of the men and 4 percent of the women have no long-range plans. About 40 percent of both men and women have college jobs that fit in "not at all" with their long-range plans, while another 22 percent have jobs that fit in "hardly at all." Fewer than one out of five students have jobs that fit in "very well" with long-range plans.

These figures show a radically different pattern if they are computed separately by type of job. Thus, for 85 percent of both the men and women with off-campus jobs in areas related to course work, the job fits in fairly well or very well with their long-range career plans. By contrast, for about 21 percent of the students with off-campus jobs in areas unrelated to course work, the job fits in either fairly well or very well with their long-range plans.

Relevance of the job to long-range plans is related to attrition in highly contrasting ways. If the student works at an off-campus job in an unrelated area, a job that fits in with long-range career plans is associated with *increased* dropout probabilities. Increases associated with a job that fits in very well, versus one that fits in not at all, are greater for women (10 percent) than for men (5 percent). For men whose off-campus job is related to course work, the pattern is reversed: a job that fits in with long-range career plans is associated with *decreased* dropout probabilities of about 8 percent. For women in such jobs, the pattern is inconsistent: increased dropout probabilities are associated with jobs that fit in very well or hardly at all with long-range plans, whereas decreased dropout probabilities are associated with jobs that fit in fairly well or not at all.

The effects of off-campus work in unrelated areas may be explained in at least two ways. If a student holds an off-campus job that could develop into a career, that student may be tempted to leave college and pursue that job full time, particularly if that career does not require a college degree. At the same time, students who find the academic going rough or who otherwise become dissatisfied with their institutions may be more tempted to drop out if they have a meaningful outside job. Perhaps the judgment that the job fits in well with long-range plans is a rationalization of the decision to drop out rather than an antecedent to that decision.

The results for men who work off-campus in areas related to course work are consistent with expectations. If the job also fits long-term career plans, the overlap between course work, job, and career is presumably maximized and the man's chances of continuing in college are strengthened. The mixed results for women, however, defy explanation. If nothing else, they underscore the need for more research into the relationship between college employment, course work, and career plans.

Job Satisfaction

On the follow-up questionnaire, students were also asked: "Consider the job which you held the longest while attending college. Did you enjoy the *kind of work* you did on this job?" The five responses, together with the percentages of men and women who endorsed each alternative, are: "No, I hated the work" (5 percent for each); "No, I rather disliked it" (18 percent and 17 percent); "I had no feelings about it" (15 percent and 11 percent); "Yes, I rather liked it" (38 percent and 39 percent); and "Yes, I enjoyed it very much" (25 percent and 29 percent). Clearly, a minority of students are employed in jobs they dislike; most students are favorably disposed toward their jobs.

Is job enjoyment related to the number of hours worked? Only slightly. The degree of enjoyment is not consistently related to the hours, although students have a slight tendency to express extreme views about their full-time jobs. They tend to be more neutral about part-time jobs.

The student's degree of job satisfaction has little relationship to persistence. Compared with men who hate their jobs, men who rather like them or like them very much have an increased dropout probability of about 4 percent. For the women, an enjoyable job makes no difference one way or the other.

Work and Marriage

Because married students are often financially independent of their parents and responsible for spouses and sometimes children as well, work represents an especially important source of support. Does work affect the married students' persistence in college? What effect does work have on students who are married when they enter college? On those who marry while they are enrolled? Four types of work during the freshman year are considered: federal work-study programs, other on-campus work, off-campus work, and work for college credit.

Federal Work-Study. Students who are married when they enter college are much less likely (about 1 percent) than single students (about 4 percent) to participate in work-study programs. Many married students work at outside jobs, a possible explanation for this underparticipation. Because of the small numbers involved, it is impossible to assess the effects of participation in work-study on students married at the time of college entry. For students who marry while they are enrolled in college, however, the rate of participation in work-study as a freshman is almost identical to that of unmarried students. Work-study participation appears to benefit married students of both sexes: for men, the associated reduction in dropout probabilities is about 7 percent; for women, about 3 percent.

Other On-Campus Employment. Once again, participation in other on-campus employment is somewhat low for students who are married at college entry (4 percent compared with 8 percent for unmarried students). Among students who marry while in college, participation is somewhat higher (about 6 percent). For these students, participation is associated with a small reduction (3 percent) in dropout probabilities for men, but no effect appears for women.

Off-Campus Employment. As expected, students who are married when they enter college are much more likely to hold off-campus jobs as freshmen (45 percent of the men and 25 percent of the women) than unmarried students (20 percent and 15 percent). For these students, holding an off-campus job is associated with large increases in dropout probabilities: 23 percent for men and 16 percent for women. For students who marry after entering college, the situation is reversed: working off campus is then associated with reductions in dropout probabilities: 9 percent for men and 5 percent for women. Reductions for unmarried students are 4 percent for men and 3 percent for women. Having an off-campus job as a freshman is a poor diagnostic sign for students who marry before college. For such students, working at an outside job may indicate extreme financial need or possibly lack of involvement in and commitment to undergraduate work.

Although the absolute numbers of black students who are married and who also hold jobs while in college are. quite small (about forty students in both the black college and white college samples participated in federal work-study, while another fifty in each sample held off-campus jobs), the results of their employment merit attention. Since too few students were married at college entry for comparison, these results are limited to students who marry while in college. For these students, both work-study and off-campus jobs are associated with large decreases in dropout probabilities averaging about 27 percent. These effects occur for both types of jobs and for blacks in black colleges as well as blacks in white colleges. Although off-campus employment and, in particular, federal work-study programs are associated with substantial reductions in dropout probabilities for both groups of blacks (see Chapter Three), their effects are much greater (more than double) among students who marry in college. While these findings should be viewed with caution because of the small samples, the magnitude of the impact suggests that employment may be a potent means to reduce attrition among black students who marry after entering college.

In short, students who marry while enrolled are more likely to finish college if they establish a pattern of employment during the freshman year. The benefits of employment are especially apparent for white men and for black students, regardless of whether they attend black or white colleges.

Work and Financial Aid

Although federal work-study programs are considered as part of traditional financial aid packages in Chapter Three, it is also possible to consider the influence of other forms of student employment on attrition when they are combined with the two principal modes of direct financial support: grants and loans.

Grants and Scholarships. Participation in federal work-study has maximum impact among students without grants or scholarships and a negative impact among those for whom grants are a minor support source during the freshman year. For the men, participation in other on-campus work as freshmen produces similar results: 8 percent reduction in dropout probabilities among men with no grant support and negligible impact among men with grant support. Results for women are quite different: an on-campus job during the freshman year is associated with a minor reduction in dropout probabilities (6 percent) among women with minor support from grants, a slight negative effect (2 percent increase in dropout chances) among women with major grant support, and a borderline reduction in dropout probabilities (1 percent) among women with no grants. Thus, among women with minor grant support, the type of on-campus employment appears to make a considerable difference. Federal work-study has a negative impact on persistence, while other forms of on-campus employment have a positive effect. This negative impact, which also occurs for men with minor grant support, may result from the packaging practices of particular institutions.

Grants combined with off-campus employment during the freshman year again produce contrasting findings for men and women. For the men, an off-campus job is associated with a 4 percent reduction in dropout probabilities among those with no grants or minor grant support and an 8 percent reduction among those with major grant support. Results for women with no grants or minor grant support are almost identical, but the outcomes for those with major grant support are strikingly different: a small (1 percent) *increase* in dropout probabilities.

Loans. The impact of participation in federal work-study programs during the freshman year is highly dependent on the amount of support the student receives from loans (see Chapter Three). Work-study reduces persistence for students who rely on loans as a minor support source yet has a substantial positive impact on those who depend on loans as a major support source. Other forms of on-campus employment have a positive influence on persistence (5 percent for men and 2 percent for women) if the student also receives major loan support, but an even greater positive impact (15 percent for men and 5 percent for women) if the student receives minor loan support.

Off-campus employment produces still different results: no significant effects for students receiving major loan support and substantial positive results for students receiving no loans (4 percent for men and 12 percent for women) or minor loan support (8 percent for men and 13 percent for women).

While the highly complex and sometimes contradictory nature of these findings makes any systematic interpretation difficult, several trends are noteworthy. To begin with, combining grants or loans with work-study produces somewhat different results from combining these forms of financial aid with other on- or off-campus work. In all likelihood, these contrasting effects are related in part to practices in packaging financial aid, whereby large support from one source (such as work-study) decreases the amount available from other sources (for example, loans or grants). Presumably, on- and off-campus employment is obtained by students more or less independent of traditional financial aid. These two forms of employment appear to facilitate college persistence among students of both sexes if they are also receiving minor loan support. The same holds true for students receiving minor grant support, with the exception of men with on-campus jobs other than work-study. All forms of work during the freshman year, including work-study, tend to be associated with reduced dropout probabilities if the student has no scholarship or loan support. The single exception to this general trend occurs among men with no loan support; for them, both forms of on-campus employment have negligible impact. In short, any form of on- or off-campus employment during the freshman year presents an opportunity to enhance the student's chances of completing college if the student is not receiving other forms of financial aid. If federal work-study programs are excluded, the same positive impact of work occurs among students who receive minor support from either grants or loans. The most unpredictable consequences of work occur among students who receive major support from either grants or loans. One possible explanation of this interaction is that, for students whose financial need is such that they require major support from either grants or loans, the additional burden of a job detracts significantly from the ability to finish college. Whatever the reason, work should be used sparingly as a device to alleviate financial need among students heavily dependent on scholarships or loans.

Summary

Clearly, the student's chances of finishing college can be significantly influenced by the type and extent of employment. The data warrant these general conclusions.

1. Having a job usually increases the student's chances of finishing college. If employment is less than full-time (under twenty-five hours a week), the absolute benefits can be substantial: from 10 to 15 percent decrease in dropout probabilities. These positive effects of employment are even more pronounced among black students.

2. In general, full-time employment is to be avoided. For most students who work full-time, the positive effects of employment on persistence are not only lost but actually reversed. The only situation in which students appear able to tolerate full-time employment occurs when men hold jobs on campus. This exception may be in part a consequence of the types of full-time jobs normally held by men on college campuses.

3. On-campus work is generally preferable to off-campus employment. However, if a student holds an off-campus job during the freshman year, the effects are generally positive. Shifting from an on-campus job or no employment to an off-campus job, however, is associated with a substantial increase in dropout probabilities.

4. The negative effects of full-time employment are especially pronounced when the student works off campus.

5. The degree of relevance of the job to the student's long-term career interests is negatively associated with persistence if the student works off campus. That is, students with off-campus jobs are more likely to drop out the more their work is related to career goals.

6. The degree of job satisfaction has little effect on persistence.

7. Entering college students who are married have less chance of finishing college if they also work during the freshman year. Employment as a freshman has a positive effect, however, if the student marries after entering college.

8. The effects of college employment are most beneficial among students who receive no grant or loan support or only minor support from these two sources of financial aid. For students with substantial financial need, packaging work programs with scholarship and loan support should be done with care. Clearly, more research into the effects of various packages is needed.

5

RESIDENCE AND CAMPUS ENVIRONMENT

Two broad classes of campus experience affect student persistence. The first is variations in the student's resident status, such as living at home, in a dormitory, or in a private room. The second includes various environmental contingencies, such as academic achievement and extracurricular activities.

Residence

Where students reside while attending college can be directly controlled by policy-makers, administrators, and students. Policy-makers who view living in college residence halls as beneficial can appropriate funds to improve or expand these facilities; those who do not hold such views can encourage the expansion or development of commuter institutions. Institutional administrators favorably disposed toward the residential experience can require or otherwise encourage students to live in dorms. Students who wish to leave home to attend college can limit their choices to residential institutions, whereas students who wish to live at home or in a private room can bypass institutions that require students to live in residence halls.

Numerous studies suggest that dormitory living enhances college persistence (Alfert, 1966; Astin, 1973; Astin and Panos, 1969; Chickering, 1974; DiCesare, Sedlacek, and Brooks, 1972; Kramer and Kramer, 1968). With the 1968–1972 longitudinal data available, the impact of college residence can be explored in greater depth with more elaborate controls over entering student characteristics.

In the 1972 follow-up questionnaire students were asked where they had lived each year since entering college in 1968. Six options were available: with parents; other private home, apartment, or room; college dormitory; fraternity or sorority house; other student housing; and other. Since few students were involved (less than 4 percent) in the last two categories, these categories were combined for the analysis.

Assessing the impact of college residence on attrition presents methodological problems similar to those encountered earlier in the analysis of financial aid and work. If a student drops out of college during, say, the second year, the possibility of living in a college dormitory after that time is precluded. To avoid artifactual correlations between residence and attrition, the initial analysis of the impact of alternative experiences considered only the student's freshman residence. The methodology was identical to that in Chapters Three and Four: actual dropout rates for students who lived in various residences were compared with expected dropout rates computed from the student's entering freshman characteristics, and from the variables of financial aid, work situation, and type of college. The multiple correlations between these control variables and dropping out are .44 and .41 for white men and women, respectively, and .42 and .59 for blacks in black and in white colleges, respectively.

Dormitories. More than half of all students (49 percent of the men and 63 percent of the women) live in a college dormitory as freshmen. The comparable percentages for black students are 69 percent for those in black colleges and 43 percent for those in white colleges. In all four samples, living in a dormitory as a freshman is associated with reduced dropout probabilities.

Although the magnitude of this impact varies somewhat from one type of institution to another (see below), living in a dormitory instead of most alternative residences as a freshman appears to decrease the student's dropout chances by approximately 10 percent.

One problem in obtaining a quantitative estimate of the benefits of dormitory living is that the proportion of students in dormitories varies markedly from one type of institution to the next. If institutions are separated into two-year colleges, four-year colleges, and universities, the proportions of men and women living in dormitories in each type of institution are: public universities (68 and 73), private universities (64 and 71), public four-year colleges (54 and 66), private four-year colleges (74 and 84), public two-year colleges (8 and 6), and private two-year colleges (39 and 62).

For most students, the principal alternatives to dormitory living are their parents' home or a private room or apartment. Comparing dormitory living with the alternatives reveals the positive impact of dormitory living on persistence. Compared with living with parents, dormitory residence during the freshman year is associated with these decreases in chances of dropping out (in percent):

	Men	Women
Public universities	−12	−11
Private universities	− 9	− 1
Public four-year colleges	−10	− 6
Private four-year colleges	−11	− 2
Public two-year colleges	+ 7	0
Private two-year colleges	−20	− 5

Although the number of black students in each type of institution is too small for similar comparisons, trends in the data for blacks are consistent with those in the data for whites.

Compared with a private room or apartment, living in a

dormitory is associated with these decreases in chances of dropping out (in percent):

	Men	Women
Public universities	−7	−16
Private universities	−3	− 7
Public four-year colleges	−5	−11
Private four-year colleges	−3	− 6
Public two-year colleges	+5	− 8
Private two-year colleges	−6	—*

* Number of students too small to compute reliable estimates.

The benefits of dormitory residence as a freshman are clear. The practical implications of these findings for students are obvious: their chances of finishing college are improved if they leave home and live in a college dormitory. For administrators and policy-makers, the findings suggest a need for reassessment. Perhaps policy-makers should reexamine current trends toward reduced allocations for construction of residential facilities and rapid expansion of commuter colleges. College administrators who control these facilities might reconsider whether abandoning required residence for undergraduates is as beneficial as some claim.

While one might conclude that institutions can expect lower dropout rates if they require freshmen to live in dormitories, dormitory living may work only for those students who opt for it. Students forced to live in residence halls may not show the same reduction in dropout chances. To test this hypothesis, institutions were sorted into three groups: those in which fewer than 10 percent of the freshmen lived in dormitories (commuter colleges), those in which between 10 percent and 90 percent lived in dormitories (voluntary residential colleges), and those in which more than 90 percent lived in dormitories (required-residence colleges). Since institutions that require residence for freshmen differ markedly in their policies about exceptions, institutions in which more than 10 percent of the freshmen did not live in dormitories were considered de facto not to have a residence requirement. The question here is whether dormitory living has a different impact on these two groups (the required and the unrequired). The expected and actual dropout rates for men and women attending the three types of institutions show clearly that the impact of campus residence is uniform; that is, the relative decrease in dropout probabilities associated with living in a dormitory versus living with parents or living in a private room is comparable in all three categories. Thus, the beneficial effects of dormitory living are not compromised by a residence requirement.

The only type of institution in which dormitory living does not have a positive impact is the public two-year college. (Astin, 1973, reports a similar finding.) This effect is largely attributable to a handful of such schools with residential facilities. Whether these colleges accurately represent the total population of public colleges offering residential facilities is unknown. Clearly, a more intensive study with a larger and more representative sample is needed of the impact of residence in public two-year colleges.

Living with Parents. The parents' home is the second most common residence during the freshman year. Percentages of the four groups who live at home are: white men (38), white women (30), blacks in black colleges (25), and blacks in white colleges (44). Since this living option has a negative impact on persistence when compared with living in a dormitory, how does living with parents compare with living in a private room or apartment? The changes in dropout percentages are:

	Men	*Women*
Public universities	+ 5	−5
Private universities	+ 6	−6
Public four-year colleges	+ 5	−5
Private four-year colleges	+ 8	−4
Public two-year colleges	+ 2	−8
Private two-year colleges	+14	—*

* Number of students too small to compute reliable estimates.

The difference between the effects for men and for women is dramatic. Regardless of type of institution, living in a private room or apartment rather than with parents is beneficial to men and detrimental to women. To speculate on these findings: For men, getting away from the home environment may facilitate greater involvement in campus and academic life. The positive results of dormitory living support this hypothesis, which is further strengthened by the finding that, for both men and women who leave home to attend college, the chances of finishing are greater if they live in dormitories rather than in private rooms or apartments. Greater involvement in campus life and activities appears to lead to greater persistence. What this explanation does not consider, however, is the apparent negative effect for women of living in a private room rather than at home.

Differences in the degree of personal autonomy and independence accorded men and women during their high school years may be a factor. For example, among 1968 college freshmen the typical man had probably already had more opportunities to be away from home and to behave independently than the typical woman. For some women, the change in dependence and autonomy between living at home and at college in a private room or apartment may be too dramatic. Without the normal controls of the typical dormitory, women living away from home for the first time in a private room may not be able to handle the interpersonal peer pressure associated with such an acute shift in degree of independence. The resulting stress not only may detract from their ability to cope with academic work but may also pressure them to leave college for the more supportive home environment.

Private Rooms or Apartments. That freshman women may be differentially prevented or discouraged from living in a private room is suggested by the percentage of men (6) versus women (3) who do so. Except for the public two-year colleges, these sex differences occur in all types of institutions. The proportions of men and women living in private rooms or apartments are: public universities (5 and 2), private universities (3 and 2), public four-year colleges (6 and 2), private four-year colleges (2 and 1), public two-year colleges (10 and 10), private two-year colleges (10 and 2).

The relatively large proportion of two-year public college students who live in private rooms and the lack of sex differences may be attributed to the lack of residential facilities, as well as to the high proportion of older and married students.

Fraternity and Sorority Houses. Although few students live in fraternity and sorority houses as freshmen (3 percent of the men and 1 percent of the women), the findings merit consideration. The only type of institution in which both sexes live in fraternities or sororities in sufficient numbers to permit comparison is the public university. For both men and women attending such institutions, living in a fraternity or sorority as a freshman is associated with a *greater* reduction in dropout probabilities (by about 6 percent) than living in a dormitory. Although these findings must be viewed with caution because the number of students involved is relatively small, they further support the involvement hypothesis; that is, living in a fraternity or sorority may carry with it even greater student involvement in peer relationships and campus social life than living in a dormitory.

Other Residences. The combination of "other student housing" and "other" accounts for the residence of 4 percent of the men and 3 percent of the women freshmen. Just what living arrangements these alternatives involve is not entirely clear, since the students did not elaborate. Possibly, married students living, independently checked this alternative, particularly if they were living in married-student housing. Because less than 2 percent were married, these students are only a minority of the respondents. Students living in coops or communes or with relatives other than parents may also be included. The expected and actual dropout rates for men in this group are similar to those for men living with their parents: an increase in dropout probabilities compared with living in a dormitory or private room. If anything, the increases are greater (1 percent to 3 percent) than those associated with living with parents. For women, the results are mixed. Among women attending private institutions (whether universities, four-year or two-year colleges)', increases in dropout rates are comparable to those associated with living with parents. For women attending public institutions the results resembled those for dormitory living; that is, a general decrease in dropout probabilities. Without further data, it is impossible to provide reasonable explanations for these findings. The results do suggest, nevertheless, that alternative forms of freshman residence are probably not associated with favorable outcomes, particularly among men. If nothing else, these data suggest the need for further research into alternative living arrangements.

Patterns During First Two Years. So far the effects of residence during the first college year have been examined. Do these effects continue beyond the first year? To avoid the artifacts already noted, a series of separate analyses was performed only for students enrolled *full-time during the first two years of college.* Limiting the sample presumably removed artifacts from the data, since students in theory could live anywhere during each undergraduate year. Only nine combinations of residential experiences during these first two years were studied, as shown in Table 11.

The relationship of persistence to each residential pattern was assessed by comparing the expected and actual dropout rates of students in each pattern with the expected and actual dropout rates for all students enrolled full time during their first two undergraduate years. The nine patterns are ranked in terms of their degree of relationship to persistence (see Table 11).

It is not surprising that continuous residence in fraternity or sorority houses or in dormitories during the first two undergraduate years is associated with increased persistence. Nor is it surprising that students who live with their parents during the first year and move into a dormitory during the second year also show increased persistence. What is perhaps unexpected is to find students who live in dormitories during the first year but with parents during the second year showing a marked increase in dropping out. Whatever benefits are gained through dormitory residence during the first year apparently are lost entirely if the student moves in with parents. What could be occurring here is not so much an effect of a particular residence, but a pattern that represents a prelude to dropping out. It is not unreasonable to suppose, for example, that students who live in a dormitory during their first college year but move in with parents during their second year have encountered unforeseen difficulties that necessitate changing their residential pattern. Since the pattern involves a movement away from the campus, it may reflect a declining interest in the collegiate environment or possibly

Table 11.

PATTERNS OF RESIDENCE DURING FIRST TWO YEARS
RELATED TO DROPPING OUT

Place of Residence		Percentages		Changes in Dropout Percentages	
First Year	Second Year	*Men*	*Women*	*Men*	*Women*
Fraternity or Sorority	Fraternity or Sorority	3	1	− 4	− 8
Dormitory	Fraternity or Sorority	7	5	− 2	− 3
Parents	Dormitory	3	3	− 4	− 1
Dormitory	Dormitory	33	53	− 2	− 1
Private Room	Private Room	4	2	− 4	+ 2
Parents	Parents	28	24	0	− 1
All Others	All Others	2	1	+ 6	+ 3
Parents	All Others	18	10	+ 3	+ 8
Dormitory	Parents	3	2	+ 18	+ 17

Note: Includes only students enrolled full time during the first two years.

a change of institutions. It is not uncommon for students to leave home for college the first year, then transfer to a local community college for the second year and live at home. Whatever the appropriate explanation, these data show dramatically that dormitory living followed by living with parents is symptomatic of a tendency to drop out.

Academic Environment

The 1972 follow-up questionnaire asked a number of questions about academic experiences. Students were asked their cumulative undergraduate gradepoint average (GPA), as well as their average grade in their major fields, whether they were ever on probation, whether they participated in honors programs, and whether they studied abroad. These experiences all have an impact on student attrition.

Performance. A student's undergraduate GPA is more closely related to persistence than any other single variable examined in this study. (Since overall GPA bears a stronger relationship to attrition than grade average in the major, the focus here is on overall GPA.) Cumulative undergraduate GPA is assessed on a seven-point scale: 3.75–4.00 (A or A+), 3.25–3.74 (A− or B+), 2.75–3.24 (B), 2.25–2.74 (B− or C+), 1.75–2.24 (C), 1.25–1.74 (C− or D+)', and less than 1.25 (D or less). The relationship between the student's overall GPA and attrition is shown in Table 12.

Clearly, academic performance is a major factor in college attrition for both men and women, as well as for blacks and whites. Practically every student with an average grade of C− or lower drops out. This relationship, of course, is to be expected, since students with GPAs below C usually are not permitted to graduate. However, the association is also strong among students with passing grades: the dropout rate for students with B averages, for example, is nearly twice that for students with A averages. While these results indicate that students' grades substantially affect motivation to stay in college, it should be added that even among students with A or A+ averages, nearly one in five drops out. High grades are therefore not the only condition for remaining in college.

To what extent can the relationship between attrition and college grades be attributed to initial differences in dropout-proneness among students at college entrance? To explore this question, the expected dropout rates were computed separately for students at each grade level. (For these analyses, the student's freshman residence was added to the other predictors to compute the expected dropout rates.) The results are shown in Table 12.

Clearly, differences in dropout rates among students with different college GPAs are attributable in part to differences in background and potential at time of college entry. The differences in expected dropout rates, however, are substantially less than the differences in actual rates, as one can see in Table 12.

The effects of academic performance on attrition cannot be attributed entirely to differences among students when they enter college. College grades appear to influence persistence directly, independent of initial variations in ability and family background, financial aid and work during college, freshman residence, and type

Table 12.

ACTUAL AND EXPECTED DROPOUT RATES OF STUDENTS
AT SIX GRADE LEVELS
(Percentages)

Gradepoint Average	Expected	Actual	Actual Minus Expected
White Men			
3.25–4.00	24	15	— 9
2.75–3.24	32	22	— 10
2.25–2.74	39	31	— 7
1.75–2.24	47	69	22
1.25–1.74	53	97	44
Less than 1.25	54	100	45
White Women			
3.25–4.00	24	19	— 5
2.75–3.24	28	23	— 6
2.25–2.74	35	34	— 1
1.75–2.24	45	72	27
1.25–1.74	48	92	44
Less than 1.25	42	100	58
Blacks in Black Colleges			
3.25–4.00	27	19	— 8
2.75–3.24	28	17	— 11
2.25–2.74	38	31	— 7
1.75–2.24	44	67	23
1.25–1.74	60	88	28
Less than 1.25	—*	—*	—*
Blacks in White Colleges			
3.25–4.00	28	21	— 7
2.75–3.24	42	28	— 15
2.25–2.74	45	39	— 6
1.75–2.24	61	72	12
1.25–1.74	66	96	30
Less than 1.25	—*	—*	—*

* Number of students too small to compute reliable estimates,

of institution. (These variables were included in computing expected dropout rates.)[1] Grades in the B range (GPA between 2.75 and 3.24) appear to have the strongest positive effect on persistence, particularly among black students. Low passing grades (GPA between 1.75 and 2.24) are strongly associated with dropping out, although the negative effect of the three lowest grade intervals is no doubt attributable in part to the inclusion among the dropouts of some students who were dismissed for academic reasons.

In one sense, these results offer further confirmation of the involvement theory: Students who are involved in the academic life of the institution are more likely to expend the effort necessary to get good grades than are students who are not involved. In another sense, the results relate to the question of fit between students and institutions: Students with mediocre or poor grades experience a lack of fit between (a) their own performance and that of most of their fellow students, and (b) their low level of achievement and the high value placed on achievement by the institution. (The question of student-institutional fit is treated at length in Chapter Seven.)

These findings raise some questions about both admissions and grading policies. Persons who object to open or otherwise relaxed admissions policies argue that the traditional selection criteria (high school grades and aptitude test scores) should be used to prevent students incapable of completing college from enrolling. If such students are admitted, the argument goes, they do not perform well enough academically to complete their studies. Clearly, higher education is a long way from identifying beforehand students who are unable to cope with the academic demands of college. Thus, of those students who end up with failing grades (and who almost all drop out), only about half were expected—according to analyses in this study—to drop out. By the same token, the prediction here is that about one in four students who get A averages will drop out (about one in five actually does). In short, the ability to forecast who will not finish college because of failing grades is limited.

---

[1] The multiple correlations of these predictors with dropping out for the four groups are: white men (.447), white women (.419), blacks in black colleges (.442), and blacks in white colleges (.591).

52760

Those who influence grading policy might consider these findings from the opposite direction. About half of those students who drop out with failing grades are predicted *not* to drop out on the basis of their entering freshman characteristics. Similarly, although the prediction is that about one-fourth of those students with A averages will eventually drop out, fewer than one-fifth actually do. In short, even considering the students' initial potential for academic performance and dropping out, their actual grades still have a pronounced impact on the decision to leave or remain in college.

Thus, a substantial number of students who show college potential on the basis of traditional admissions criteria drop out because of grades. In addition, a much smaller but significant number of students who do *not* exhibit the potential for academic achievement get high grades and consequently complete their studies. These imperfections in the ability to predict who will succeed in college suggest that academic administrators would be well advised to examine the importance of grades as a motivating factor. For the student with college potential who does not perform well, there may be some advantage to modifying grading procedures or at least withholding grades until the student has had an opportunity to make them up.

Probation. One technique that institutions commonly employ for students with poor academic records is to place them on "academic probation," a grace period during which students have an opportunity to improve their academic performance.

As expected, there is a strong relationship between undergraduate gradepoint averages and being placed on probation (in percent):

	Men	*Women*
3.25–4.00	3	1
2.75–3.24	9	6
2.25–2.74	32	22
1.75–2.24	56	42
1.25–1.74	60	58
Less than 1.25	55	43

Why men should be on academic probation more frequently than women is not clear. One possible explanation is that, within each grade interval, the men have slightly lower grades than the women. It is also of interest that students with the lowest gradepoint averages are slightly less likely to be placed on probation than those in the next-to-lowest category (1.25–1.74). Conceivably, students with mostly failing grades simply leave college without going through the interim step of academic probation. Also, such students may simply be dismissed from the institution, while students with a few passing grades may instead be put on probation and given a chance to improve the poorer grades.

To assess the impact of academic probation on student persistence first requires a control for college grades, since grades can directly affect attrition whether or not the student is on probation. Expected and actual dropout rates were computed for students who were and were not on academic probation, separately by levels of GPA. The changes in dropout percentages associated with being placed on academic probation are shown below:

	Men	*Women*
3.25–4.00	20	−13
2.75–3.24	7	5
2.25–2.74	0	− 9
1.75–2.24	− 3	1
1.25–1.75	7	− 9
Less than 1.25	− 4	—*

*Number of students too small to compute reliable estimates.

These data suggest that the effects of being placed on academic probation are not the same for men and women. Although the patterns are not entirely consistent, there is some tendency for academic probation to increase the men's chances of dropping out and to decrease women's chances. If it is true that women place a higher value than men on academic achievement, probation may be interpreted by women more as a challenge and may motivate them to remain in college and try to bring their grades up. More men, on the other hand, may interpret probation as a sign of failure and may consequently become discouraged and drop out. While these interpretations are admittedly speculative, the empirical data indicate that the possible motivating effects of being placed on academic probation merit a great deal more careful study. If nothing else, probationary status should be used judiciously with undergraduate men.

Honors Programs. Honors programs represent a polar counterpart to academic probation. Usually, student participation in honors programs is based on demonstrated academic potential or achievement, a bias illustrated by the close association between participation (in percent) and cumulative GPA:

	Men	*Women*
3.25–4.00	35	30
2.75–3.24	19	14
2.25–2.74	6	6
1.75–2.24	2	2
Less than 1.75	0	0

Contrasting the expected and actual dropout rates of participants and nonparticipants at each grade level reveals these associated changes in dropout percentages:

	Men	*Women*
3.25–4.00	− 1	− 2
2.75–3.24	− 3	− 2
2.25–2.74	− 2	−17
1.75–2.24	−25	—*
Less than 1.75	—*	—*

* Number of students too small to compute reliable estimates.

Participation in honors programs is uniformly associated with improved chances of college completion. Though honors programs may offer a promising method to reduce attrition (particularly among students with lower GPAs), a note of caution about possible methodological artifacts is in order. Since many students do not participate in honors programs when they enroll but become involved later, it is possible that the apparently positive effects occur because students who leave college before graduation have fewer opportunities to participate in honors programs, regardless of GPA. Since students with lower grades are more likely to leave college than those with higher grades, this artifact would tend to produce (as above) larger effects among students with less outstanding grades.

   Credit by Examination. Proponents of nontraditional higher education programs have long advocated greater use of certification by examination. Opponents of this form of awarding credits argue that such credits are not really comparable to those earned through traditional course work and therefore compromise academic standards. Advocates assert that the student's academic progress is facilitated by this means and that carefully controlled examinations actually ensure better quality control over performance standards than traditional course grades. Regardless of the merits of such arguments, an important empirical question is whether this means of certification actually facilitates the student's chances of completing college.

   Eleven percent of the men and 13 percent of the women receive some form of credit by examination while enrolled as undergraduates. (The percentages for blacks are somewhat lower: 7 percent of those in black colleges and 8 percent of those in white colleges.) Comparison of expected and actual dropout rates indicates that receiving credit by examination is significantly associated with college persistence. The associated reduction in dropout probabilities for white students is 5 percent for both men and women; for black students it is somewhat larger: 12 percent for blacks attending black colleges and 11 percent for blacks attending white colleges. While the artifact mentioned above must be considered— that is, the longer the student stays in college, the greater the chances of receiving credit by examination—the results suggest that credit by examination may offer another potential means to reduce student attrition.

   Foreign Study. In the follow-up questionnaire, students indicated whether they had studied abroad for a term or longer as an undergraduate. Relatively small percentages of students had done so: 2 percent of the white men and 5 percent of the white women, and less than 1 percent of blacks at black colleges and 3 percent of blacks at white colleges. Opportunities for study abroad seem extremely limited for blacks in black colleges.

Data on expected and actual dropout rates reveal a positive association between foreign study and student persistence. The associated reduction in dropout probabilities is 3 percent and 8 percent, respectively, for white men and women, and 11 percent for blacks attending white colleges. Again, one difficulty is the artifact: the longer a student remains in college, the greater the opportunity to study abroad. Thus, the findings on foreign study should be viewed with caution.

A related question concerns foreign travel that may or may not involve foreign study. On the follow-up questionnaire students were asked whether they had traveled or lived abroad between 1968 and 1972. A substantially higher proportion of the students said they had: 16 percent of the white men, 22 percent of the white women, 7 percent of the blacks attending black colleges, and 13 percent of the blacks attending white colleges. In general the results of such exposure follow the patterns for foreign study.

When expected and actual dropout rates are compared, foreign travel (which may or may not involve study) is shown to be *negatively* associated with student persistence. The resulting increases in dropout probabilities are 8 percent for both the white men and women, and 7 percent for blacks attending black colleges. No significant effect appears among blacks attending white colleges. When the students whose foreign travel also involves formal study are excluded, these negative effects of foreign travel are even larger.

That travel abroad should be associated with increased dropping out is to be expected, since such travel normally consumes time and detracts from the normal academic routine and environment. In a sense, these data provide still more support for the involvement hypothesis. One might argue, of course, that here is a reverse artifact; that is, if a student drops out of college, the probability that the student might subsequently travel in a foreign country is increased. Whether or not this is the case, the magnitude of these associations suggests that foreign travel that does not involve formal study should be regarded as a potential obstacle to completing college.

Extracurricular Activities

Any attempt to assess the relationship between persistence and student participation in extracurricular activities is handicapped by the artifact that the longer a student stays in college, the greater the opportunity to participate in extracurricular activities. To reduce the effects of the artifact, analyses of the impact of extracurricular participation were limited in two ways. First, only those students enrolled full-time during the first two undergraduate years were included. Second, two extracurricular activities—participation in varsity sports and membership in social fraternities or sororities— were selected to the exclusion of other possibilities (for example, participation in choir, glee club, band, drama society, college paper or literary magazines, and honorary societies). These two activities were chosen because, under normal circumstances, students who become involved in them do so during the first two years. Few students, if any, join social fraternities or sororities or become members of varsity teams after the sophomore year.

As expected, participation in athletics among blacks in white colleges (17 percent) is higher than that among blacks in black colleges (12 percent). The comparable rate for white students is 13 percent (18 percent for men and 6 percent for women). Membership in social fraternities or sororities is surprisingly high among all groups. Some 38 percent of both white men and women join such organizations; among blacks attending black colleges, the percentage is even higher (47 percent), and among blacks attending white colleges, the percentage is comparable to that for whites (39 percent).

The methodology to assess participation in varsity athletics or social fraternities or sororities is identical to that used to assess patterns of residence during the first two years. Actual and expected dropout rates of participants are compared with actual and expected rates for all students enrolled full-time for the first two years. The results offer further confirmation of the involvement hypothesis. Participation in varsity athletics reduces chances of dropping out by 1 percent for white men and 5 percent for white women and blacks in white colleges. Membership in fraternities or sororities is associated with even further reductions, from 6 to 9 percent for all four groups. The only exception to these trends occurs among black students who participate in varsity athletics at black colleges. For them, participation is associated with a small increase in dropout probabilities (about 2 percent). Conceivably, the intense athletic competition at black colleges detracts from the positive effects of greater involvement in campus activities.

Summary

1. A student's chances of completing college can be significantly influenced by environmental circumstances. The positive effect of living in a dormitory during the freshman year has obvious implications for students, administrators, and policy-makers. Students concerned about maximizing their chances of finishing college should seriously consider leaving home and living in a college dormitory. Simply getting away from home appears to enhance a man's chances of finishing college even if he lives in a private room or apartment. For the woman, however, leaving home may reduce her chances of finishing college if she opts for private residence.

2. The student's GPA is strongly related to persistence, more so than any other student variable in this study. That grades, however, do not always indicate the student's academic potential is reflected in the fact that many students with high potential drop out and many with presumably low potential manage high grades and stay in college. Putting students with poor grades on academic probation appears to have positive effects on women and negative effects on men.

3. Participation in honors programs by the high achiever is associated with a modest decrease in dropout probabilities. Foreign study is also associated with reduced chances of dropping out, but foreign travel without formal study is substantially related to increased dropout probabilities.

4. Participation in extracurricular activities, especially membership in social fraternities or sororities, is also significantly related to staying in college. These findings support the theory that student persistence to some extent depends on the degree of personal involvement in campus life and environment.

6

CHARACTERISTICS
OF THE COLLEGE

The nearly three thousand institutions that make up the American system of higher education are an exceedingly diverse group. They differ not only in such salient attributes as size and geographic region but also in academic quality, religious affiliation, sex composition, and cost. The relationships between these institutional characteristics and student persistence also vary.

The obvious beneficiary of information about the effects of college characteristics on persistence is the prospective student. Persons choosing a college are often faced with a bewildering array of alternatives. Should I attend a large or a small college? Should it be publicly or privately controlled? Should it be coeducational or single sex? Should it be a two-year college, a four-year college, or a university? Does the region in which the college is located make any difference?

A less apparent but nevertheless important group of potential consumers of information about the impact of college characteristics is the policy-makers or planners at the municipal and state level. This group, which includes legislators and legislative analysts as well as members and staffs of city and statewide governing boards, usually has responsibility for planning and developing multi-institutional systems of higher education. Typically, such persons must decide what types of new institutions should be developed and how existing institutions might be expanded or otherwise modified. A related policy question concerns coordination between private and public higher education and the degree of public support available to institutions in the private sector.

Since the focus here is on the student's institution, variations in the expected and actual dropout rates of institutions are examined. The range of actual dropout rates among the 358 institutions in this study is indeed remarkable: from a 3 percent low to an 81 percent high. Expected dropout rates also vary widely, although the range is slightly attenuated. As it happens, the two institutions with the highest and lowest actual dropout rates also have the highest and lowest expected rates. If only estimates of dropout-proneness are used, the expected rates for these institutions are 13 percent and 61 percent. If the estimates also include measures of financial aid, work status, and freshman residence, the expected rates are 9 percent and 65 percent—another step nearer to the actual rates. If measures of the various college characteristics below are also added to the estimates, they come still closer: 5 percent and 75 percent. As expected, actual dropout rates correlate highly with these three estimates: .78, .83, and .91. In short, institutions vary widely in their actual dropout rates, and much of this variation can be attributed to the characteristics of their students at the time of college entry.

The institution with the lowest dropout rate (3 percent) is a highly selective, private-nonsectarian liberal arts college for women located in the Northeast. Of all types of institutions, private-nonsectarian colleges and Catholic women's colleges of high selectivity (mean freshman SAT verbal and mathematical above 1,250) tend to have the lowest dropout rates: the mean dropout rate of the twenty-seven institutions in this category that participated in the study is only 13 percent. Other institutions with relatively low mean dropout rates are the selective universities (18 percent) and selective Protestant colleges (19 percent). Not surprisingly, these institutions generally have many of the student and environmental qualities associated with persistence: a highly able and highly motivated freshman class, few married students, a high proportion of Jewish students, dormitory facilities (often with required residence for freshmen), large internal resources for financial aid, and many opportunities for on-campus employment. While the dropout rates of these private colleges may seem low, students who left their first college before completing the baccalaureate were not counted as dropouts in the current study if they persisted at some other college.

The institutions with the highest dropout rate (81 percent) are both two-year colleges: one a private college located in the South, and the other a large public college located in the West. Of all types of institutions, the public two-year or community colleges consistently show the highest dropout rates (mean of approximately 59 percent). Rates are somewhat higher—about 65 percent—at two-year colleges located in the West and Southwest. In contrast to the selective universities and private colleges, the public two-year college typically has student and environmental attributes associated with dropping out: students who are of relatively low ability and relatively unmotivated, few Jewish students, high proportions of married students and older students, no residential facilities, limited job opportunities and limited financial-aid resources, and few opportunities for extracurricular activities.

The findings here concern the relationship between student persistence and a variety of institutional characteristics: type of college (two-year versus four-year versus university), control (public versus private), religious affiliation, sex (coeducational versus single sex), geographic region, selectivity (level of prestige), size, and cost.

Type and Control

College type and control are characteristics that occupy a central position in the thinking of legislators, planners, and policy-makers. The three types of institutions are administered in separate tiers in the public system of some states (such as California), whereas in other states these distinctions are blurred. Similarly, the public-private dichotomy frequently influences legislative and policy decisions at the national and state levels. The differential problems of private versus public institutions, for example, often affect state scholarship programs and public subsidy to private institutions.

Because of these considerations, institutional type and control are combined here, resulting in six categories of institutions. These are shown in Table 13, together with data on expected and actual dropout rates. The actual dropout rates of the first four types of institutions, public and private four-year colleges and universities, are substantially lower than those of public and private two-year colleges. Indeed, the dropout rates of the public two-year colleges are nearly three times those of the private universities. However, considering differences in the dropout-proneness of the entering students (Table 13, two center columns), many differences among the six types of institutions appear much smaller. As a matter of fact, for public universities, the expected dropout rates based on entering student characteristics are almost identical to actual rates.

Even after controlling for differences in student dropout-proneness, however, substantial effects of institutional type remain. Attending a public two-year college rather than a private university increases the student's dropout chances by about 16 percent, substantially less, of course, than the differences in actual dropout rates: 36 percent and 38 percent, respectively, for men and women. The relatively high dropout rates of the two-year colleges can be attributable partially to the relatively high dropout-proneness of their entering students.

One might argue with some justification that the differences in dropout rates which remain after differences in dropout-proneness have been controlled in part result from other environmental circumstances rather than something inherent in the institutions themselves. Students attending two-year colleges, for example, are much less likely to live in residence halls. In addition, they probably have less access to financial aid and on-campus jobs. Chapters Three, Four, and Five indicated that these three circumstances—financial aid, work, and dormitory residence—can enhance the students' chances of finishing college. If environmental circumstances are also controlled, do differences in expected and actual dropout rates still obtain?

To explore this question, a new set of expected dropout rates was computed which included not only the estimates of student

Table 13.

IMPACT OF COLLEGE TYPE ON STUDENT ATTRITION
(Percentages)

Institution	Actual Dropout Rate		Actual Minus Expected Dropout Rate			
			Student Dropout-Proneness Only		Student Dropout-Proneness, Freshman Residence, Financial Aid, and Work	
	Men	Women	Men	Women	Men	Women
Public universities ($N = 46$)	33	27	0	−1	1	0
Private universities ($N = 30$)	20	21	−6	−2	−5	−2
Public four-year colleges ($N = 38$)	31	25	−5	−4	−4	−4
Private four-year colleges ($N = 181$)	27	24	−6	−3	3	3
Public two-year colleges ($N = 42$)	56	59	10	14	5	9
Private two-year colleges ($N = 21$)	54	45	9	4	8	5
Protestant ($N = 52$)*	29	31	−4	1	—	—
Roman Catholic ($N = 47$)*	23	23	−7	−5	—	—

* Also included in first six institutional types listed above.

dropout-proneness, but also measures of the student's financial aid, work situation, and freshman residence.[1] The last two columns in Table 13 indicate the difference between these new expected rates and the actual dropout rates. Note that these additional controls reduce the negative impact of the public two-year colleges by about 5 percent for both men and women. Clearly, the negative effect of such institutions may be attributed in part to these other environmental factors. By far the most important variable here is the lack of residential facilities.

Controlling for additional environmental circumstances had a pronounced effect on the results for one other type of institution, the private four-year college. Reductions in dropout rates (6 percent for men and 3 percent for women) which appeared when only student dropout-proneness was controlled changed to *increases* in dropout probabilities (3 percent for both sexes) when residence, financial aid, and work variables were controlled. These findings warrant two conclusions: first, the private four-year college has greater resources in residence halls, financial aid, and work opportunities than any other type of institution. Second, when the effects of these specialized resources are controlled, attendance at a private four-year college appears to *increase* slightly the student's chances of dropping out. As a matter of fact, for students who have equivalent financial aid, work opportunities, and residence, attending a public two-year college rather than a private four-year college increases dropout chances only slightly (2 percent for men and 6 percent for women).

In maximizing the chances of completing college, the public four-year institution appears by far the best "buy." Within the public sector, state colleges improve the student's chances of persisting by about 5 percent compared with the universities and by about 10 percent (9 percent for the men and 13 percent for the women) compared with the two-year colleges. The only type of institution with a comparable outcome—the private university—is, of course, much more expensive than the typical public four-year college. For students who can bear the additional cost of the private

[1] The multiple correlations of these predictors with dropping out for the four samples are: white men (.415), white women (.406), blacks in black colleges (.437), and blacks in white colleges (.572).

university, however, the greater prestige usually associated with such institutions may be worth the additional expense.

Why the public four-year colleges should facilitate student persistence is not immediately apparent. One possibility is that the academic demands of such institutions are somewhat less than those of public universities and substantially less than those of private four-year colleges. However, this interpretation is not consistent with results for the private universities, whose academic demands presumably are equivalent to those of the private colleges.

The private four-year colleges may fare poorly in relation to their counterparts in the public sector because of their relative isolation and more limited curricular offerings. The effect of institutional size (below) supports this explanation.

Religion

Although initially most private colleges were founded by religious denominations, the majority today no longer have formal ties with any church. This secularization of private colleges has been particularly marked within the Protestant denominations; most Roman Catholic colleges still maintain some formal affiliation with the founding religious order.

Roman Catholic institutions are by far the largest single church-related group. Although it would be informative to study separately the colleges affiliated with various Protestant denominations, their numbers were not sufficient to permit reliable comparisons. Thus, the various Protestant-affiliated institutions were combined, with the recognition that many important differences may have been confounded. Women were slightly more likely than men to attend a religiously controlled institution: 15 percent of the freshman men of 1968 and 19 percent of the freshman women attended such an institution. Protestant institutions accounted for 10 percent and 12 percent, respectively, of the men and women, while Catholic institutions accounted for 5 percent and 7 percent.

Actual and expected dropout rates for students attending religiously controlled institutions are shown in Table 13. Clearly, these colleges and universities, and in particular those associated with Roman Catholicism, have substantial holding power for their students. Since most of these institutions are four-year colleges, these results contrast markedly with results for four-year colleges as a whole. Apparently, the slight negative effect on persistence within the four-year institutions is accounted for entirely by the nondenominational colleges.

Several explanations for the positive effects of religious institutions are possible. In all likelihood, many have strong traditions that may create a close-knit, highly supportive atmosphere. Also, since most students attending these institutions come from appropriate religious backgrounds (see Chapter Seven), family and personal values are probably mutually reinforcing. Finally, earlier studies (Astin, 1968; Pace, 1974) suggest that such institutions stress academic values less than do nonsectarian colleges and, instead, emphasize community and cohesiveness. Such a pattern of environmental influence might reduce the chances of dropping out.

Coeducation

While many private and public colleges were originally founded as single-sex institutions, the number has declined rapidly in recent years and coeducation has become nearly universal. In the public sector, coeducation is virtually mandated by federal and state laws. In the private sector, however, coeducation has been stimulated largely by economic factors and, in some instances, by pressure from students.

Among the college freshmen of 1968, 9 percent of the men and 12 percent of the women enrolled at single-sex colleges. Since that time, these percentages have almost certainly declined considerably. The dropout rates for men and women attending single-sex institutions are as follows (percentages):[2] actual (28 and 23), expected (27 and 25), actual minus expected (1 and −2). Thus, attending a single-sex institution has little effect on student persistence. The effect is a little greater, however, when it is compared with coeducation, which is associated with an *increase* of about 1 percent in women's chances of dropping out. The net gain in at-

[2] In this and subsequent analyses, expected dropout rates were computed from data on residence, financial aid, and work, as well as entering student data.

tending a women's versus a coeducational college, therefore, is about 3 percent.

The small but statistically significant reduction in dropout rates among women attending women's colleges, reported earlier (Astin, 1964; Astin and Panos, 1969), may be mediated by marriage. Undergraduate women attending coeducational colleges probably have more opportunities to marry than women attending women's colleges. Since marrying after college entry is associated with increased chances of dropping out among women, one would expect the actual dropout rates at the women's colleges to be somewhat below the predicted rates.

Another possible explanation for the positive effects of attending a women's college may be the environment. Previous studies (Astin, 1968) have shown that, compared with coeducational colleges, the environments of colleges for women differ in a number of respects. Women's colleges, usually below average in size, tend to have selective admissions policies. Their student bodies tend to be highly cohesive and more cooperative than competitive, in sharp contrast to those of the men's colleges. Students also feel that the college shows a good deal of concern for the individual and that school spirit is high.

In short, the dropout rates at single-sex colleges are substantially lower than those at coeducational institutions: 28 percent for men at men's colleges versus 38 percent for men at coeducational colleges, and 23 percent for women at women's colleges versus 32 percent for women at coeducational colleges. For the men, these distinctions may be attributed entirely to differences in initial dropout-proneness, residence, work, and financial aid. For the women, they may be attributed only in part to such factors.

Geographic Region and Transferring

To assess the impact of geographic region on student persistence, the sample institutions were divided into four regions: Northeast, Midwest, South, and West and Southwest.

One problem in comparing geographic regions is that different types of institutions are not equally distributed. In the western states, on the one hand, public institutions (and, in particular, two-year colleges) predominate. In the northeastern states, on the other hand, private institutions account for a much larger share of the total enrollment. Thus, the effects of geographic region are examined separately for institutions of different type and control, as shown in Table 14.

Clearly, students attending institutions in the West and Southwest are more likely to drop out than would be expected from their characteristics at the time of college entrance. This outcome may be attributed only in part to the high concentration of public two-year colleges in this region. Note that the public universities in the West and Southwest have a slight negative effect on persistence among both men and women, although public universities nationally have a negligible effect. Also, the positive effect of public four-year colleges nationally (Table 13) does not occur among men attending institutions in the West and Southwest. This regional effect, reported earlier (Astin, 1973), may reflect more permissive attitudes toward student attrition in the Western states or it may indicate that students who leave the public universities have fewer institutional options in the private sector than dropouts from public universities in other regions.

Another potentially important aspect of regional differences concerns the effects on persistence of transferring. The 1972 follow-up questionnaire asked students whether they had attended more than one undergraduate institution. When the actual and expected dropout rates of students who did and did not attend more than one college are compared separately by type of institution within regions, an interesting pattern emerges. Nationally, for students initially enrolling at four-year colleges and universities, transferring is generally associated with a substantial increase (average of about 10 to 15 percent) in their chances of dropping out. (For students initially enrolling at two-year colleges, the effect is, of course, reversed, since transferring is the only means by which they can complete baccalaureate degrees.) But this negative effect is most pronounced in the Northeast and Midwest, somewhat weaker in the West and Southwest, and virtually nonexistent in the South. The only type of institution in which transferring is uniformly associated with increased dropout chances, regardless of the region, is the four-year private college. Students who initially enroll at such col-

Table 14.

ACTUAL MINUS EXPECTED DROPOUT RATES FOR STUDENTS IN DIFFERENT GEOGRAPHIC REGIONS
(Percentages),

Institution	Northeast		Midwest		South		West & Southwest	
	Men	Women	Men	Women	Men	Women	Men	Women
Public universities	7	−3	−1	−1	1	−1	3	3
Private universities	−6	0	−4	−4	−2	−3	−4	−2
Public four-year colleges	−7	−6	0	0	−4	−6	1	−4
Private four-year colleges	−6	−1	0	0	−7	−3	−1	4
Public two-year colleges	7	12	−5	8	10	−3	12	8
Private two-year colleges	10	6	1	2	11	6	—	—
All institutions	−2	−1	−2	0	0	−2	7	4

Note: Positive values mean dropout rates are greater than expected based on students' initial dropout-proneness, financial aid, work, and residence. Negative values mean dropout rates are below expectation.

leges increase their dropout chances by transferring, although the effect is substantially greater among men (average of 16 percent increase in dropout chances) than among women (7 percent increase). In all likelihood, these poor results for students who transfer from private four-year colleges account in part for the slight negative effect of such institutions on persistence (Table 13).

Transfers from public four-year colleges and universities produce the greatest regional differences. Transferring from public institutions in the northeastern states increases dropout chances by about 15 percent, in contrast to about 10 percent in the Midwest, 5 percent in the West and Southwest, and no increase in the South. Transferring from public institutions in the South was, in fact, associated with a decrease of about 2 percent in dropout chances.

In short, these results suggest that the higher education systems in various regions of the country differ markedly in their capacity to deal with the transfer student. Transfers have the best prospects of finishing college in the southern states and their poorest chances in the Northeast. Apparently, institutions in the Northeast (and, to some extent, those in the Midwest) are relatively unreceptive or otherwise ill-equipped to accommodate transfers from the public four-year colleges and universities.

Selectivity

"Institutional selectivity" is defined as the average academic ability of the students enrolled in a particular institution. Selectivity is an important institutional attribute because it is regarded by many not only as an index of academic quality, but as an indicator of prestige or position in the institutional hierarchy (Astin, 1972b; Astin and Lee, 1971).

Estimates of institutional selectivity were obtained from an earlier study (Astin, 1971) that utilized entrance scores of incoming freshmen. All tests (such as the American College Test and the National Merit Scholarship Qualifying Test) were converted to a common score: the sum of the verbal and mathematical portions of the College Entrance Examination Board's Scholastic Aptitude Test (SAT). Seven levels of selectivity were defined as shown in Table 15.

Table 15.

SELECTIVITY AND STUDENT PERSISTENCE

Institutional Selectivity Level	Mean SAT Verbal plus Mathematical for Entering Freshmen	Percentage of Students from Entering Population Enrolled in Each Level		Actual Dropout Rate		Actual Minus Expected Dropout Rate	
		Men	*Women*	*Men*	*Women*	*Men*	*Women*
7	Above 1235	4	3	12	10	− 3	1
6	1154–1235	10	8	23	17	0	3
5	1075–1153	12	15	27	18	− 2	− 2
4	998–1074	20	28	29	24	− 3	− 4
3	926– 997	17	19	36	35	− 3	1
2	855– 925	8	8	49	40	4	0
1	Below 855	7	6	49	42	1	1
Unknown		22	14	54	52	4	7

No estimates of selectivity were available for approximately 20 percent of the institutions. Since independent evidence (Astin, 1971) indicates that more than 90 percent would fall in the bottom two levels if test data on their entering students were available, institutions with unknown levels may be regarded as of low selectivity.

The percentages of students who initially enrolled in institutions at each selectivity level are shown in Table 15. If the students attending institutions of unknown selectivity are added to the bottom two levels, a positively skewed distribution emerges in which the majority of students attend institutions of middle selectivity while only a minority attend institutions of high selectivity. Note that men are more likely to attend institutions at the extremes of selectivity, whereas women are more concentrated in the middle levels (3, 4, and 5).

As expected, the percentages of actual dropouts, both men and women, closely parallel the various selectivity levels (Table 15). The dropout rates at the unknown selectivity level are actually higher than those at the lowest known level, perhaps partly because two-year institutions are concentrated in the category (Astin and Lee, 1971). Subtracting expected rates (based on dropout-proneness, financial aid, work status, and freshman residence) from actual rates produces the percentages shown in Table 15. The positive values for the lowest and unknown selectivity levels indicate that the actual dropout rates of institutions in these levels are somewhat higher than the expected rates, probably because virtually all the two-year colleges fall into these lowest levels.

These results are consistent with those of earlier studies reporting the positive effect of college selectivity on student persistence (Astin, 1972a; Astin and Panos, 1969; Nelson, 1966; Wegner and Sewell, 1967). However, the correlation may be entirely attributable to the negative effect of institutions at the lowest selectivity levels. Indeed, the only consistently positive effects for men and women occur at the middle selectivity levels (4 and 5).

To examine the effects of selectivity in more detail, institutions were separated by type and the effects of selectivity studied within each type. As anticipated, the correlation between selectivity and persistence largely disappears when two-year colleges are considered separately. The universities and four-year Protestant colleges evidence a slight correlation; the other types of institutions do not.

In summary, college selectivity is positively related to student persistence, but the relationship may be attributed largely to the two-year colleges, almost entirely of low selectivity, which have a negative effect on persistence. Among the four-year colleges and universities, selectivity has no systematic relationship to persistence, after controlling for the dropout-proneness of entering freshmen, their financial aid, work status, and residence.

Institutional Size

Institutional size is a characteristic of considerable concern to policy-makers as well as to prospective students. Planners and policy-makers are continuously searching for information about "critical size": that enrollment large enough to permit a variety of curricular choices as well as efficient operation, but not so large as to be unnecessarily bureaucratic and impersonal. For the prospective student, decisions are based on a trade-off between the curricular diversity and national prominence of the larger institutions, on the one hand, and the personal attention and collegiate environment of the smaller institutions, on the other. To assess the effects of institutional size, the 358 institutions were separated into eight size categories. These categories, and the percentages of the 1968 freshmen enrolling at institutions in each group, are in Table 16.

Table 16.

EFFECTS OF INSTITUTIONAL SIZE ON STUDENT PERSISTENCE

Enrollment Size	Percentage of Total Population Enrolled		Actual Minus Expected Dropout Rates	
	Men	*Women*	*Men*	*Women*
More than 20,000	8	10	− 5	− 3
10,001–20,000	20	18	2	2
5,001–10,000	18	15	0	− 1
2,501– 5,000	20	20	1	− 3
1,001– 2,500	18	17	− 1	0
501– 1,000	8	11	− 2	− 1
201– 500	3	5	12	9
Less than 201	6	4	12	7

Most freshmen enter colleges with enrollments between 1,000 and 10,000 students. That fewer than 10 percent of the freshmen matriculate in colleges with more than 20,000 students, of course, results from the relatively small number of such institutions in the country.

Subtracting expected dropout rates from actual rates for students at colleges of different sizes produces the percentages in Table 16. Small colleges having enrollments below 500 have a negative effect on student persistence. This somewhat unexpected finding runs contrary to the folklore about the beneficial environment of the small, intimate institution. These results may be attributed in part to the large proportion of institutions of low selectivity, including several two-year colleges, among the small institutions.

With the exception of these small institutions, the effects of size are inconsistent for men and women. For undergraduate men, the large institutions appear to have negative effects on persistence; for women attending such institutions, the effects are positive. Apparently, there is no magic level beyond which size becomes dysfunctional in terms of student persistence.

To gain a more in-depth understanding of the effects of size and selectivity, institutions in each size category (above) were further sorted by selectivity level, a refinement that produced some notable results. Among institutions of moderately large size (5,000–20,000 enrollment), selectivity has a consistently positive relationship with student persistence for both men and women. Among institutions of relatively small size (1,001–2,500), the relationship of selectivity to attrition is completely curvilinear; that is, institutions of moderate selectivity seem to facilitate student persistence, whereas institutions of either high or low selectivity seem to have a negative effect. Although it is difficult to interpret these findings, one result should be stressed: regardless of size, institutions with low selectivity levels appear to have a negative effect on student persistence. In large part, this effect may be attributed to the two-year institutions.

Costs

The relative cost of attending different types of institutions is a principal consideration for decision-makers. Prospective college students, of course, are concerned about keeping the costs down without sacrificing educational quality. Institutional administrators and trustees, particularly those in private institutions, face the annual conflict between raising enough tuition income to meet rising costs and keeping tuition low enough to attract students and to avoid alienating incumbents. Policy-makers at the state and national level confront a variety of conflicts over tuition: Should access to public higher education be increased through low tuition? Should those who benefit pay a greater share of the costs? How should policy-makers handle the threat to private higher education posed by the expansion of low-tuition public institutions? How can spokesmen for public and private higher education reconcile their differences over the role of tuition in calculating student financial need?

Proponents of various views about tuition policy sometimes invoke contrasting arguments about the relationship between tuition and student persistence. Defenders of low tuition argue that minimizing the financial burden of students will maximize their chances of completing college. Some who assert that students should pay a greater share of the costs maintain that students may tend to value their higher education less if it is free and that some degree of financial investment or sacrifice is motivation to keep them in college.

To explore these contrasting views empirically, institutions were separated into three categories by annual tuition. The percentages of freshmen entering institutions in each category are in Table 17. As is shown, men are more likely to enter institutions

Table 17.

TUITION AND STUDENT PERSISTENCE

Tuition Level	Percentage of Freshman Population Enrolled		Actual Minus Expected Dropout Rate	
	Men	*Women*	*Men*	*Women*
Low ($499 or less)	21	20	3	3
Moderate ($500–$1,499)	67	64	1	− 1
High ($1,500 or more)	13	16	− 3	0

charging moderate tuition and women are slightly more likely to enter institutions with high tuition. To assess the impact of tuition on student persistence, actual and expected dropout rates were compared separately within institutions at each tuition level. Expected dropout rates were based on the student's financial aid, work status, and freshman residence, as well as on estimates of dropout-proneness. The actual minus expected dropout rates, in percent, are in Table 17.

The positive values for both men and women attending colleges with low tuition mean that the dropout rates for these students are about 3 percent higher than expected. This negative effect may be attributed in part to the larger proportion of public two-year institutions within this category. For the men, tuition level appears to have a direct positive effect on persistence, with men attending high-tuition institutions having dropout rates some 3 percent below expectation. For the women, the relationship is less clear. The only significant deviation from expectation occurs among the low-tuition institutions.

These results fail to support the contention that moderate or high tuition is an obstacle to completing college. However, one must recognize that comparisons of institutions at different tuition levels confound other institutional attributes such as type and control.

To control for confounding institutional characteristics, an additional series of regression analyses was performed in which all measures of college characteristics (including tuition and institutional type) were included in the same analysis. In the regressions for white men and women, tuition did not have a significant weight, which means that, once other institutional characteristics are controlled, tuition is not associated with persistence. However, when these analyses were repeated for both samples of black students, high tuition had a significant *negative* effect on persistence, particularly among blacks attending black colleges. The negative outcome among blacks attending white colleges was borderline.

Summary

Decisions about the relative virtues of different types of institutions should be tempered by an awareness that the institutions have different resources and facilities that can influence persistence. These include financial aid, work opportunities, and residence halls. This chapter has assessed the effects of institutional characteristics independent of such resources.

1. The type of institution can have a significant impact on the student's chances of completing college. Students maximize their chances by attending a private university in any region or a public

four-year college located in the northeastern or southern states. They minimize their chances by attending a two-year institution.

2. Institutions of all types located in the western states appear to have dropout rates higher than expected. Whether this effect may be attributed to the relatively small size of the private sector in this region, to some cultural phenomenon indigenous to the West, or to some other environmental factor is not known.

3. Attending institutions with either Roman Catholic or Protestant affiliations appears to increase the student's chances of completing college. For women (but not men), attending a coeducational institution appears to increase dropout chances slightly.

4. Institutional selectivity is positively associated with student persistence, particularly among institutions of moderate size. However, this effect may be attributed largely to the uniformly low selectivity of the two-year colleges. Attendance at moderately selective institutions appears to minimize dropout chances.

5. Small institutions (fewer than 500 students) have dropout rates uniformly higher than expected. Otherwise, size shows no consistent relation to persistence.

6. Although high tuition seems positively associated with persistence, this effect may be attributed largely to the high concentration of public two-year colleges among the low-tuition institutions. Once other institutional characteristics are controlled, tuition has no direct relation to attrition.

7

MATCHING STUDENT
AND INSTITUTION

The folklore of higher education abounds with anecdotes highlighting the importance of student-institutional "fit." Most stories concern the "culture shock" experienced by students from limited backgrounds who enroll at highly selective or sophisticated institutions: the poor student at a college attended mostly by students from well-to-do families or the valedictorian from a small-town high school who is just an average student in college. While these anecdotes make interesting reading, little evidence supports or refutes them.

The question of student-institutional fit is important to a variety of decision-makers. Prospective college students, of course, are interested in choosing their institutions to maximize whatever benefits they expect from higher education. Institutional administrators wish to recruit and select the student applicants best qualified to capitalize on the particular educational programs of the institution. Policy-makers and planners responsible for multiinstitutional systems are concerned about designing differential admissions policies that will maximize the particular outcomes toward which they are directed. At the multicampus level, the issue of student-institutional

128

fit is basically sorting students most efficaciously among existing units in the system.

Most studies that have dealt with the fit or match between student and institution suffer from important methodological limitations. Research on fit is difficult because two independent variables are being studied simultaneously—an institutional variable (say, tuition and fees) and a student variable (say, parental income). Both variables can independently affect an outcome such as student persistence. The problem with studying the fit between two variables such as these is in showing that any given *combination* produces results different from those that would be expected from the independent contribution of each. In statistical parlance, variables that act in combination rather than independently produce *interaction effects*. Most earlier studies of student-institutional fit failed to distinguish between interaction effects and the independent effects of the variables that are supposed to be interacting.

A simple hypothetical example using the two variables, tuition and parental income, illustrates the problem. Say that a high versus low tuition (ignoring parental income) is associated with a 6 percent reduction in dropout probabilities. Then assume that a high versus low parental income (ignoring tuition) is also associated with a 6 percent reduction. If these two variables operate independently with no significant interaction effect (that is, no question of fit), then the 6 percent reduction associated with high versus low tuition should occur across all levels of parental income, and, conversely, the 6 percent reduction associated with high versus low parental income should occur regardless of tuition. Thus, if there is no interaction effect the poor student (low parental income) at the expensive institution should have a 6 percent better chance of finishing college than a comparable poor student at a low-tuition institution. However, if the poor student does not get the same 6 percent benefit as the wealthy student from attending a high-tuition institution, then this evidence would indicate the presence of an interaction effect between institutional cost and student wealth. Few studies of fit have been designed so that such interactions can be distinguished from the independent effects of different variables.

In other words, an adequately designed study of student-institutional fit requires that variations in student characteristics be studied in conjunction with variations in institutional characteristics. Simply showing that variation in a student characteristic such as parental income is related to attrition in one particular college or type of college does not necessarily indicate fit: Would the same income relate differently to attrition in a different college? Similarly, showing that a particular type of student (for example, low income) is more likely to drop out of one type of college than another (for example, high cost versus low cost) is also inconclusive: Would other types of students (middle or high income) do the same? What is required, in short, is data on different types of students attending different types of institutions.

The question of student-institutional fit is considered here from six perspectives. These combinations of student and institutional characteristics have been selected to measure several principal ways in which a given student's characteristics might deviate from the norm of the institution. The student characteristics (with associated institutional characteristics in parentheses) are parental income (tuition), education of father (selectivity), ability (selectivity), size of home town (size of college), family religion (religious affiliation), and race (institutional race).

Parental Income and Tuition

Chapter Six indicated that moderate or high tuition does not, as some policy-makers contend, have a negative impact on student persistence. The modest negative impact of low tuition, particularly among men, can be attributed largely to the effects of the public two-year colleges (most with low tuition). Once these effects are removed, tuition at any level has no direct effect on persistence among white men or women. High tuition does, however, appear to have a negative effect on persistence among blacks.

Is the effect of tuition uniform for students at different income levels? Supporters of low-tuition policies would probably argue that the beneficial effects of low-cost higher education on student persistence would be greatest among students in the lower income brackets. Under these circumstances, assessing the impact of tuition on students in general might well obscure such effects among the low-income students.

Another way to regard the interaction between tuition and parental income is in terms of culture shock. For example, poor students who are able to attend expensive institutions because of financial aid or other outside support may find themselves surrounded by students from affluent backgrounds. What are the effects of this combination on the low-income student's persistence? Would the student have a better chance to succeed at a less expensive college?

To explore these questions, institutions were separated into the tuition categories used earlier: low (less than $500), moderate ($500–1,499), and high ($1,500 or more). Students were also separated into three groups by parents' income: low (less than $10,000), middle ($10,000–19,999), and high ($20,000 or above). Table 18 shows the distribution of students of various income levels

Table 18.
PARENTAL INCOME AND COST OF COLLEGE
(Percentages)

Annual Tuition Fall 1968	Parental Income					
	Men			Women		
	Low	Middle	High	Low	Middle	High
High ($1,500 or more)	8	13	27	8	16	34
Medium ($500–$1,499)	68	66	63	69	63	57
Low ($500 or less)	24	21	10	23	21	9
Total	100	100	100	100	100	100

by college tuition. Notice that about two-thirds of the students at all income levels enroll at medium-tuition colleges. Substantial differences by income levels, however, occur in attendance at high- and low-tuition institutions. High-income students are three to four times more likely than low-income students to attend high-tuition institutions. Low-income students, however, are twice as likely as high-income students to attend low-tuition colleges. Middle-income students fall in between, although they are generally closer to the low- than to the high-income students.

To assess the possibility of an interaction between income and college costs, actual and expected dropout rates for each of the eighteen groups in Table 18 were compared. In this case, the expected rates were calculated from all predictor variables: student dropout-proneness; financial aid, work status, and freshman residence; *and* college characteristics (including tuition, college type and control, religious affiliation, coeducation, selectivity, and size).

These analyses produced radically different results for men and women. Among low-income students, attending a high- rather than a low-tuition institution reduces dropout chances for men (by about 3 percent) and *increases* dropout chances for women (by about 2 percent). Among high-income students, however, a reversal occurs. For high-income men, attending a high- rather than a low-tuition institution is associated with an *increase* in dropout chances of about 5 percent, whereas among women it is associated with a *decrease* of about 6 percent. Among high-income men, the results at medium-tuition institutions are similar to those at low-tuition institutions (that is, a 4 percent decrease in dropout rates compared wth high-cost institutions). Among high-income women, results for medium-tuition institutions resemble those for high-cost institutions: a decrease in dropout chances of about 8 percent.

While these results are statistically significant, the relatively small percentage differences suggest that they should be viewed with caution. Nevertheless, they provide possibilities for speculation: Women, apparently, follow the culture shock theory, with the woman from the low-income family performing rather poorly in the expensive institution. Women from high-income families perform relatively well if they attend a high- or medium-cost rather than a low-cost institution.

For men, the results are exactly reversed. Why the low-income man should perform better in the high-cost than in the low-cost college, and why the high-income man should perform better in the low- and medium-cost rather than the high-cost colleges is not clear. One possibility is support and encouragement from parents, variables not directly measured in this study. Is it possible that boys from low-income families who manage to gain acceptance at high-cost colleges receive an unusual degree of encouragement and support from the family? Is it possible that among low-income families this form of upward social mobility represents a more highly valued goal for boys than for girls?

Another possibility is financial aid. Since definition of the amount of the student's stipend is relatively crude ("major" versus "minor" support)', it is possible that low-income men attending expensive colleges receive large stipends. Thus, even though an attempt has been made to control for financial aid, the control may have been inadequate because high- and low-income students may have different definitions of what constitutes major versus minor support. Similar definitional differences might exist between students in high-cost and students in low-cost institutions. Earlier evidence (Astin and Christian, 1975) revealed substantial differences in the size of scholarship stipends received by men and women attending high-cost colleges. If nothing else, these possibilities indicate that the interrelationships among financial aid, parental income, college cost, and sex merit closer study.

Selectivity and Parental Education

Another way of looking at the culture shock phenomenon is in terms of parental education rather than income. For this purpose, the father's educational level is used as a measure of the student's cultural background and selectivity is used as a measure of the overall cultural level of the institution. Since there was no available measure of the average educational level of the students' fathers, selectivity became a kind of surrogate institutional measure. Earlier research (Astin, 1962, 1965) showed that institutional selectivity is highly correlated with the average educational level of the students' parents.

If selectivity level 4 (mean SAT verbal and mathematical of 1,000 or above) is arbitrarily chosen as the dividing line between selective and nonselective colleges, the percentages of students attending selective institutions by father's educational level are as follows:

	Men	Women
Postgraduate degree	67	69
College degree	62	62
Some college	47	53
High school graduate	42	49
Some high school	39	42
Grammar school or less	29	37

The relationship between probability of attending a selective college and father's educational level is strong. Students whose fathers have a postgraduate degree are about twice as likely to attend a selective college as students whose fathers have only a grammar school education or less. The relationship appears somewhat stronger among men than among women.

To explore the interaction between these two variables, the relationship between selectivity levels and attrition was computed separately within each level of father's education. The resulting patterns are rather strange, but consistent for both men and women. In general, the positive association observed in Chapter Six between selectivity and persistence is strong among three groups: those whose fathers had some high school, were high school graduates, or had postgraduate degrees. A large part of the relationship is accounted for, of course, by the low selectivity of the two-year institutions. Associations are less clear cut among two of the remaining three groups, those whose fathers had only a grammar school education and those whose fathers were college graduates. In the group whose fathers had some college education, the relationship is actually *reversed:* the association between college selectivity and persistence is slightly negative. Why the children of college dropouts show a unique pattern with respect to college selectivity is not immediately clear. Possibly the knowledge that the father was a college dropout may condition the student's response to the college environment. Is it possible that the presence of a large number of students whose fathers had successfully completed college may prove threatening to students whose fathers were college dropouts? While these speculations may be farfetched, this unique relationship suggests the need for further research into the motivational characteristics of undergraduates whose parents were college dropouts.

Selectivity and Student Ability

The relationship between student ability and college selectivity is perhaps one of the most crucial for decision-makers. Those who defend selective admissions policies argue that only the brightest students are able to take full advantage of the substantial resources of the selective institution, and that the less able students will be intimidated and frustrated by heavy academic demands. Proponents of more open admissions policies argue that the resources of the more selective institutions should be available to all students and that, with appropriate remedial and supportive services, even those of low ability can profit from exposure to the rigorous environment of the more selective institutions. Selective admissions, they argue, is a denial of equal educational opportunity.

Institutional administrators and faculty usually favor selective admissions policies because an academically elite student body enhances institutional prestige. Also, institutional personnel—most of whom have already demonstrated their ability to deal effectively with traditional academic material—find the more able students easier to identify with and to teach. That minority of personnel that favors relaxation of normally selective admissions policies argues that institutional resources should be available to a wider range of students. Opponents of relaxed admissions cite lowered academic standards and the high costs of remedial and counseling programs.

Students also have a large stake in the relationships between selectivity and ability. Does the student of moderate or low ability have any chance of success at a highly selective institution? Is the high-ability student who attends the nonselective institution handicapped in educational development?

These student-oriented questions have substantial significance for policy-makers as well. Is a track system, in which freshmen are sorted among institutions according to ability, the most efficacious in maximizing each student's chances of completing college? Would a more homogenized system, in which institutions do not differ greatly in selectivity, produce a better overall result? Are the effects of a more homogeneous system different for high- versus low-ability students? Such questions have implications for planning in multiinstitutional city and state systems.

To explore the possible interaction between student ability and institutional selectivity, students were arbitrarily divided into three categories by scores on standard college admissions tests. Using the SAT as a guide, the three ability categories are high (SAT verbal plus mathematical above 1200), average (between 825 and 1200) and low (below 825). Since college students are superior to the general population in ability, these terms should be viewed in their relative rather than absolute sense. The cutting point between low and average ability falls at about the 20th percentile, while the cutting point between average and high ability falls at about the 85th percentile (Astin, 1971) for college freshmen nationally.

The percentage distribution of high-ability students by institutional selectivity level is shown below:

	Men	*Women*
7	95	93
6	92	90
5	69	65
4	20	16
3	9	8
2	8	7
1	3	5
Unknown	4	9

The most selective institutions are attended almost exclusively by high-ability students, but there are, nevertheless, some high-ability students in the least selective institutions. Unfortunately, for purposes of analysis, the converse is not true of low-ability students. Thus, among institutions in the top three selectivity categories, not even one-half of 1 percent of the students are of low ability. By contrast, about one-third of both men and women entering colleges in selectivity level 1 are in the low-ability group. Thus, the current distribution of students among institutions precludes any study of the low-ability student in the highly selective institution. This combination occurs too infrequently to produce sufficient cases for analysis. Indeed, in the most selective colleges (level 7), the proportion of students of average ability is perilously low for a reliable comparison.

To further assess the interaction between student ability and college selectivity, the expected and actual dropout rates of students at each ability level were compared separately within each category of selectivity. Expected dropout rates were based on financial aid, residence, and work predictors, as well as estimates of dropout-proneness. The most consistent findings occur among students attending institutions in the top three selectivity groups. Among both men and women in these institutions, the high-ability students drop out somewhat more often than predicted and students of average ability drop out somewhat less often. The effect is especially pronounced in the top selectivity level, where the relative advantage, in terms of reduction in dropout percentages, for the average- versus high-ability students is 10 percent for the men and 22 percent for the women. These findings fail to support the widely held belief that highly selective institutions are ideally suited to the educational needs of the most able students. On the contrary, the interaction effect is precisely the reverse: the highly able student drops out more often than predicted and the average student less often than predicted. This conclusion should be tempered, however, by a recognition that the average student in the highly selective institution may possess positive attributes not reflected in the battery of 110 student input measures.

Findings for students in the other selectivity groups suggest additional interaction effects but reveal no rational pattern. At selectivity level 3, for example, there may be a positive interaction with ability for the men: the higher the ability level, the greater the relative advantage for the men (the relative advantage for high- versus low-ability men in this selectivity category is a reduction in dropout percentages of 10 percent). For the women at selectivity level 3, however, the effect is reversed: *low*-ability women have about an 11 percent advantage over high-ability women.

Among students attending institutions in the unknown selectivity group, which includes a large proportion of junior colleges, those of either high or low ability appear to have an advantage over those of average ability. The advantage seems especially great among the men: 31 percent for low-ability and 17 percent for high-ability men. However, at selectivity level 1, where a higher proportion of four-year colleges and universities are found, the situation is again reversed: average ability has an advantage over low ability (6 percent for the men and 1 percent for the women) and high ability (13 percent for the men and 5 percent for the women).

While such findings defy explanation, a number of general conclusions seem warranted. First, no consistent evidence supports the widely held beliefs that students of high ability are penalized by attendance at nonselective institutions and that students of average ability are ill-suited to highly selective institutions. Second, ability differences are more important for men than for women attending nonselective institutions. Finally, the inconsistent interactions suggest that additional studies to examine ability-selectivity interactions separately within different institutional categories (for example, four-year private liberal arts colleges) may be necessary before consistent patterns emerge.

Size of Home Town and Size of College

The size of the student's home town and the size of the college form another relationship where the fit between student and institution may be important. Presumably, students who were raised on farms or in small towns are less well prepared to deal with the interpersonal stresses and bureaucratic procedures of large, complex institutions than students who have grown up in large cities. At the same time, one might argue that the student from the large city is less well prepared to deal with the intimacy and lack of urban stress typical of the small college.

If such hypotheses are valid, one might expect students to gravitate toward colleges with environments that resemble the towns where they lived most of the time while growing up. To explore this possibility, the percentage of students attending colleges with enrollments of 5,000 or more was computed separately by size of home town:

	Men	*Women*
Farm	36	33
Small town	34	29
Moderate-size town or city	40	40
Suburb of large city	57	50
Large city	60	62

The size of the home town *is* related to the size of the college. Students from large cities and suburbs are about twice as likely to attend a large institution as students from farms and small towns. Similar differences are evident in the percentages attending small colleges with enrollments of less than 1,000: 27 percent of the men and 29 percent of the women with farm backgrounds, compared with only 11 percent of the men and 17 percent of the women from large cities.

To explore the interaction between size of home town and college size, actual and expected dropout rates were computed for students attending colleges of different enrollments separately within each home-town category. Expected rates were based on all predictor variables: estimates of dropout-proneness based on entering student characteristics, financial aid, work status, and freshman residence; and college variables, such as size, selectivity, type, control, and religious affiliation. Deviations under these circumstances presumably would be the result of interactions between size of home town and size of college.

In general the results support the hypothesis about fit between home-town and college size but only at the extremes of college-size categories. Thus, in the large institutions (enrollment over 20,000), students from farms and small towns have dropout rates higher than expected. The differences are substantial: 9 percent for both men and women who come from farms, and 4 percent and 19 percent, respectively, for men and women who come from small towns. Students from moderate-size or large cities attending institutions with enrollments over 20,000 show the opposite effect. Among those from moderate-size cities, actual dropout rates are 5 percent and 10 percent lower than expected, respectively, for men and women; among students from large cities the differences are 7 percent and 3 percent, respectively, for men and women.

These interactions are largely reversed among students attending small institutions. Students from large cities, for example, have dropout rates (13 percent for men and 5 percent for women) higher than expected when they attend institutions enrolling fewer than 500 students. Similar discrepancies (10 percent for men and 6 percent for women) occur among students from the suburbs of large cities who attend small colleges. The results for students from farms and small towns tend to show the opposite pattern, although data are not entirely consistent. Among students from farms who attend small institutions (enrolling fewer than 200 students), drop-out rates are lower than expected (3 percent for men and 13 percent for women). In the next-to-smallest size category (200–400), however, no such results are obtained with students from farms (in fact, the dropout rates are higher than expected by 17 percent for men and 4 percent for women). Students from small towns and moderate-size cities show no particular pattern of interactions in the small colleges.

In short, the fit between the size of the student's home town and the college is important to student persistence. Students from urban backgrounds do substantially better in the large institutions than do students from farm or small-town backgrounds. Students from large cities and suburbs, however, fare poorly in small institutions. It must be stressed that size differences over a wide range (enrollments between 500 and 20,000) show no consistent interaction with home-town size.

Religion

Another potentially important aspect of student-institutional fit is religious affiliation. The best fit presumably would be experienced by a student whose religious background matched his institution's religious affiliation. Does this compatibility enhance student persistence? Do students with atypical religious preferences find themselves in a foreign or hostile environment that prompts them to leave?

Religiously affiliated institutions enroll only a minority of students, as we have seen earlier, and those who do attend such institutions often have religious preferences consistent with the institution's affiliation. Thus, less than 1 percent of non-Catholic students attend Catholic institutions, compared with 14 percent of Catholic men and 20 percent of Catholic women. In fact, the numbers of students whose religious backgrounds are Jewish, other, or none are so small in Roman Catholic institutions that the sample is insufficient to examine interaction effects.

Attendance at Protestant institutions is not quite as extreme.

Thus, the proportions of men and women of different religious backgrounds who enroll at Protestant institutions are: Catholic (3 percent of both men and women), Jewish (8 percent of men and 4 percent of women), "other" (10 percent of men and 14 percent of women), and none (6 percent of men and 7 percent of women). For Protestant students, the percentages are 15 for men and 20 for women.

To examine the possible interactions between religious background and institutional religious affiliation, expected and actual dropout rates were compared separately within various student-institutional combinations. Expected dropout rates were computed using all variables, including institutional characteristics.

The results tend to support the importance of student-institutional religious fit. Among Protestants attending Roman Catholic institutions, for example, dropout rates are substantially higher than expected (10 percent for the men and 3 percent for the women). Protestants attending Protestant institutions, however, have a slight advantage (2 percent for men and 1 percent for women). Roman Catholic students attending Protestant institutions do not show similar negative interactions. In fact, their dropout rates are slightly lower than expected (1 percent for men and 2 percent for women). Apparently, it is easier for the Roman Catholic student to adjust to the Protestant institution than for the Protestant student to adjust to the Roman Catholic institution. One possible explanation is that the Roman Catholic student does not find the environment of the typical Protestant college as foreign as the Protestant student finds the environment of the typical Catholic college.

Jewish students evidence some notable interaction effects. For Jewish men, attending a Protestant institution is associated with an increase in dropout probabilities of about 6 percent. For Jewish women, the results are reversed: their dropout rates are some 15 percent lower than expected (this finding must be viewed with caution because the sample was relatively small, about forty women). Any incompatibility between Jews and Protestants may be greater among men than women.

Results for students of "other" religious backgrounds also produced contrasts for men and women. Among men attending

Protestant institutions, dropout rates are about 10 percent *lower* than expected. Among women, the results are reversed: dropout rates are about 11 percent higher than expected.

Students who checked "none" as their religious background tended to produce results similar to those for Jewish students: men from such backgrounds attending Protestant colleges show dropout rates higher than expected (by about 13 percent), whereas women show rates lower than expected (by about 7 percent). Again, these results must be viewed with caution because of the small samples.

Jews and students with no religious background also produce similar findings in the private nonsectarian institutions, many of which were formerly Protestant.

In summary, several important interactions are present between student religious background and institutional religious affiliation. In general, Protestant students persist better than students from other religious backgrounds in Protestant institutions and worse than Roman Catholic students in Catholic institutions. Among men, those from Jewish backgrounds or no religious background drop out more often than students from "other" religious backgrounds in the Protestant colleges and the private nonsectarian colleges. Among women from Jewish backgrounds and no religious background, precisely the opposite occurs: they fare somewhat better than women from "other" religious backgrounds in the Protestant and private nonsectarian colleges. Evidently, acceptance of students from deviant religious backgrounds (including agnostics or atheists) is greater in the Protestant colleges among women than among men.

Race

In American higher education, most racially homogeneous institutions are predominantly black colleges. A major decision for any black prospective student is whether to attend one of these institutions or a predominantly white institution where blacks represent a small minority. What are the consequences of this decision for the black student? Are the chances of becoming a dropout influenced by this choice?

The higher dropout rates for blacks in white colleges (49.5

percent versus 37.0 percent for blacks in black colleges) suggest that attending a white college may handicap the black student's chances of finishing. At the same time, one might argue that this difference is not a college effect but rather an effect of differences in the dropout-proneness of black students entering the two types of institutions.

One approach to this issue is to simulate the results one would have obtained if the black students attending black colleges had attended white colleges and, at the same time, if the black students at white colleges had attended black colleges. The most direct method is to apply the regression weights used to estimate the dropout-proneness of one group to the other and to compare this new set of expected dropout rates with actual rates. If the same factors operated to influence blacks in black colleges and in white colleges, the two sets of weights would produce the same expected dropout rates for any given group. Among blacks attending white colleges, a revised expected dropout rate of 32.8 percent was obtained using the weights from blacks in black colleges. The actual dropout rate for these students (49.5 percent) is about 17 percent higher, suggesting that the black student's chances of finishing college are substantially reduced by attending a predominantly white college. Reversing the procedure for blacks in black colleges produces similar findings. When the weights obtained from the blacks in white colleges are applied to those who attended black colleges, the expected dropout rate is 46.5 percent. This is nearly 10 percent higher than the actual rate for these students (37.0 percent), suggesting that persistence among black students is facilitated by attending a black college.

A number of explanations for these apparent interactions between student and college race are possible. One might argue, on the one hand, that the academic demands of the black college are substantially fewer than those of the white college. That this is probably not an appropriate explanation is suggested by the data in Chapter Six, which did not support the hypothesis that college selectivity has a negative effect on persistence among blacks attending white colleges. Indeed, the dropout rates are somewhat higher than expected among blacks attending white colleges of *low* selectivity. The most favorable outcomes for blacks in white colleges are associated with attending an institution in the middle ranges of selectivity.

Another possible explanation is the isolation and alienation that many blacks students feel in a white college. In this regard, note that these students entered college at a time (fall 1968) when black militance was nearing its peak in many white institutions. This militance, together with associated white backlash, may have fostered strong feelings of alienation among these black students which prompted many to drop out. In all likelihood, the environment of predominantly white institutions today is much different. Whether or not these differences will result in better persistence rates among blacks attending white colleges can only be determined by additional research.

Although it would have been equally productive to examine the impact of attending predominantly black colleges on white students, their numbers were much too small for any reliable assessment. It was possible, nevertheless, to gain further insight into the findings for black students by applying the weights used to estimate dropout-proneness among black students attending white colleges to the white students in those colleges. These additional analyses show that the expected dropout rate for white men using these weights is somewhat higher than the actual rates: 41.4 percent versus 36.8 percent. Differences for white women are substantially smaller: an estimated rate of 31.7 percent versus an actual rate of 30.9 percent. The negative effects of attending white colleges are substantially greater for black men than for black women, a finding which supports racial conflict and alienation as one reason for an attrition rate higher than expected for blacks at white colleges. That is, since racial conflicts and protests more often involve men than women, one would expect to find sex differences if racial conflict is among the underlying causes for high attrition among blacks in white colleges.

Summary

After examining the fit between student and institution, it appears that, in general, persistence is enhanced if the student attends an institution in which the social backgrounds of other students resemble his or her own social background. Such interactions are most apparent with the town size, religion, and race of the student.

Contrary to popular belief, evidence on the interaction between student ability and institutional selectivity does not show that students persist better if they attend colleges with students of similar ability. This finding raises a serious question about the usual educational justifications for ability tracking and selective admissions in public and private institutions.

8

IMPLICATIONS FOR DECISION MAKING AND RESEARCH

Throughout, this volume has reported findings of particular relevance to decision-makers. In this concluding chapter, these various findings are pulled together in concise summaries directed at three major groups of decision-makers—institutional administrators, educational policy-makers, and students—and then at scholars interested in future research on college dropouts.

Because this study focuses intensively on the single outcome of student persistence in college, the following suggestions and recommendations are based implicitly on the assumption that these decision-makers want to minimize students' chances of dropping out. It goes without saying, of course, that almost any decision must simultaneously weigh other outcomes for which no data are presented here: for example, other aspects of the student's development (satisfaction with the college, knowledge gained from the educational experience, and so forth), as well as the relative cost of

146

different alternatives, possible side effects of each, and the constraints operating in the decision process. The consumer of these findings need not necessarily assume that dropping out is always detrimental to all students. There are cases where the student's personal development is clearly enhanced by leaving college. What this study does assume is that large numbers of administrators, policymakers, and students have a legitimate interest in understanding the personal and environmental circumstances that lead a student to drop out of college and that they may wish to alter these factors to maximize the student's chances of finishing.

Several qualifications about the following recommendations should be kept in mind. First, the recommendations are not necessarily applicable to all types of students attending all types of postsecondary institutions. The data were obtained from full-time students enrolling for the first time in traditional collegiate institutions. Students who aspire only to an associate degree or to no degree were excluded.

Second, some findings may not apply to students who are married at college entry. Although in a few instances it is possible to point to specific factors that influence married students differently from single students, the small number of married students precluded a full-scale separate study of them. In contrast, students were studied separately by sex and race, and all results that apply uniquely to men or women as well as to black or white students are noted.

Third, while most of the following recommendations apply both to public and private universities and four-year and two-year colleges, the special problems of community colleges and other types of commuter institutions will be considered separately wherever appropriate.

With these qualifications in mind, the recommendations below should provide decision-makers with a better empirical basis for choosing alternatives to minimize student dropout rates.

Institutional Decisions

Persons in institutions who are in a position to make decisions that influence students' chances of completing college include most administrators and many faculty members, as well as staff members in offices of admissions, financial aid, placement, housing, and counseling. Previous chapters provide strong evidence that these groups make choices which significantly influence dropout rates.

Most of the following recommendations focus on student involvement in the institution. If ways can be found to involve students more in the life and environment of the institution, their chances of staying in college are improved. A number of mechanisms are available to most institutions to bring about greater student participation: academic programs, admissions, freshman orientation, counseling and advisement, financial aid, work opportunities, extracurricular activities, and housing and student services.

Academic Programs. The student's undergraduate grade-point average has a stronger relationship to dropping out than any other single variable. Even when the student's prior academic background and ability are taken into account, college grades relate strongly to dropping out. This relation is not simply an artifact of policies that force students with low grades to leave college. Indeed, with ability controlled, those with B averages are substantially less likely to drop out than are students with C+ averages. Thus anything that can be done to enhance students' academic performance will also tend to reduce attrition rates.

The possible intervention techniques are numerous: tutoring, programmed instruction, special courses for developing study skills, and self-paced learning, among others. Institutions can, with relatively little investment of resources, carry out controlled experiments on a limited scale to identify the most promising approaches. With well-designed studies, the more effective techniques in raising students' performance can be identified within a short time—say, within one term after initiating the study.

One major clue to the importance of academic factors that lead to dropping out is contained in the reason students give most frequently for leaving college: boredom with courses. Both men and women cite this reason more often than poor grades; and it is, in fact, the single reason given most frequently by men. While boredom may be a socially acceptable rationalization for leaving college, it also indicates noninvolvement. That it is a factor in dropping out is consistent with other evidence which reveals lack of involvement as a critical element in the decision to leave college. In these circumstances, institutions would be well advised to undertake studies of reasons for student boredom, including poor teaching, uninterest- ing courses, superfluous requirements, and so forth. If student bore- dom could be reduced or minimized, many students who become dropouts might well remain in college.

At least two specific types of intervention programs may directly affect student persistence: participation in honors programs, and credit by examination (the latter being particularly related to persistence among black students). While limitations in the data require that the relationships be viewed as tentative, a rational case for the potential value of both is easy to make. In honors programs, students are singled out for special attention, a practice that may have substantial motivating effects. In credit by examination, stu- dents are permitted to accelerate their undergraduate education to avoid the usual lockstep sequence of courses spread over four years. Credit by examination to recognize competencies acquired outside traditional course work has been attempted on a large scale, with apparent success, in a few institutions, such as Empire State College, and deserves greater use.

One technique used by many institutions to provide border- line students with an opportunity to improve their academic per- formance is academic probation. Results of the current study on the impact of probation on persistence in college are equivocal, how- ever. They suggest a positive effect on persistence among women and a negative effect among men. Since the data are not consistent, the need for more research, particularly by individual institutions on the effect of their own probation policies, is apparent.

While it may seem facetious to suggest that the most direct approach to improving students' academic performance is simply to award higher grades, such a change is not entirely out of the question. Indications are that the grading practices of undergradu- ate institutions have changed substantially during recent years in terms of an upward shift in average grades. Whether this trend is in turn reducing attrition remains to be seen.

The principal objections to awarding higher grades are two- fold: academic standards are compromised, and any motivating effects of high grades are sacrificed because the entire grade dis- tribution shifts upward. Nonetheless, academic standards can be controlled directly at the level of certification as well as by grades. Students can be required to demonstrate desired levels of competence either through senior examinations or comprehensive evaluations administered at various points in the undergraduate years. As long as these standards are defined and maintained, one could, in theory, have any grading system that proved effective in motivating students to study and to stay in college. In other words, institutions can introduce radical innovations in their grading systems and still maintain academic standards.

Whether the positive motivating effects of high grades would be lost if the number of low grades were reduced is an empirical question that can only be resolved through systematic research. Considering the apparent potency of grades as a motivator to leave or stay in college, institutions can legitimately justify systematic studies of the impact of alternative systems.

One alternative to awarding higher grades is not to award grades to students who are performing poorly, or to allow them more time to improve performance to the point where higher grades can be awarded. Other possibilities can include substituting a low C for failing and allowing self-grading. Even if no changes in the grading system are introduced, institutions can still experiment with the other techniques mentioned above to improve the students' academic performance. Of course, if such techniques are effective, the net result will be to raise the overall grade distribution.

Finally, study in a foreign country appears to be an academic program—albeit an expensive one—that can reduce student attrition. Travel abroad without any formal academic course work, however, clearly increases the chances of dropping out, as do departmental programs that involve some form of employment for credit. Largely because they frequently require full-time work off campus, such programs have a uniformly negative effect and should be avoided.

Admissions. The admissions process can also minimize student attrition in several ways. Many institutions can and do select students primarily to minimize dropout rates, and a somewhat crass approach is simply to pick students whose dropout-proneness (see Chapter Two and Worksheets at the end of the book) is low. Aside from the serious ethical and legal problems posed by this method, admitting only the least dropout-prone students would really not affect the individual student's chances of persisting in college. The net result of such a policy among selective institutions would be nil as far as national dropout rates are concerned.

Perhaps most important in terms of setting admissions policy is the finding here that the ability to predict dropping out is still extremely limited. Using all the best predictor variables from this study as admissions criteria would make possible only a moderate improvement in predictive accuracy. Thus, a substantial proportion of the most dropout-prone students admitted would complete their program and a small but significant number of the least dropout-prone students would not finish theirs. In short, institutions can be much more flexible in their selective admissions without fear that dropout rates will be unduly influenced.

This study found no systematic interaction effect between student ability (or dropout-proneness) and college selectivity, an important corollary finding. Contrary to the popular belief that only the brightest students can survive in the highly selective institutions, or the opposite theory that the bright student will be penalized by attending a less selective institution, the few students of moderate ability who enter highly selective colleges do better than expected on the basis of their entering characteristics. Possibly the highly selective institutions could admit more such students without fear that their dropout rates will greatly increase.

In considering changes in admissions policy, institutions should keep in mind that a number of *environmental* circumstances can also influence attrition rates. Thus, if an institution that normally provides housing for its freshman class decides to increase substantially the number of commuter students who are admitted, the dropout rates for these additional students are likely to be relatively high. Other examples of changes in admissions that would tend to be accompanied by higher attrition rates would be increases in the number of students who work at outside jobs full time, in the number of men who have to rely on support from loans, or in the number of women who will be living away from home but cannot be housed in residence halls. (Whether the women's movement will bring changes in these relationships is a question for future researchers to consider.)

Perhaps the major educational justification for selective admissions is that certain types of people (those who are selected) are better able than others (those who are rejected) to benefit from an institution's academic offerings. Despite the wide range of variables in this study, little evidence justifies such an assumption. The only plausible support derives from the relationship between institutional size and the size of the student's home town. In general, students from urban homes persist better in large institutions (enrollments above 20,000) than students from farms or small towns. At the same time, students attending small institutions (enrollments below 500) persist better if they are *not* from a large city. Although these data suggest that overall dropout rates could be reduced if students from farms or rural backgrounds were discouraged from attending large institutions and students from urban backgrounds were discouraged from attending small institutions, whether such results justify the use of home background as a selection criterion is another matter. If nothing else, institutions at the extremes of the size continuum should understand that the home backgrounds of their students may be critical to their ability to persist in college.

Orientation. Student orientation sessions can be utilized in at least two ways to reduce attrition rates. First, students can be familiarized with the findings of this study and the factors in their own background and in their environment which affect their dropout chances (where they live, whether they hold a job, whether they marry, and so forth). Providing students with such information would better enable them to elect environmental options that would help them complete college.

Second, orientation sessions could be used to collect data from individual students to assist in computing estimates of dropout-proneness. At a minimum, such information would include the items in the Worksheets at the end of the book. Institutions could also conduct research to obtain more accurate estimates.

One application of such survey data would be to calculate the expected dropout rate for any new class of entering students to determine immediately whether it differs from preceding classes. Information that the new class is substantially more dropout-prone would be valuable in adjusting enrollment projections for subsequent years. It could prompt institutions not only to step up recruitment, but also to make more vigorous efforts to reduce the projected high dropout rate of that class. If the survey indicated a significant decline in dropout-proneness for a new group of incoming students, this information too would be useful in planning facilities and revising enrollment projections.

Estimates of dropout-proneness could also give institutions a more realistic basis for evaluating their own dropout rates. Many institutions with relatively high dropout rates have been unfairly criticized because their detractors have failed to consider the initial dropout-proneness of their students. At the same time, colleges with relatively low dropout rates are sometimes given too much credit for an outcome that is partly the result of having entrants whose dropout-proneness is relatively low. The point is that both types of institutions can obtain much more realistic self-appraisals by comparing expected and actual dropout rates. (See also the discussion of evaluation procedures in the later section on implications for policy-makers.)

Counseling and Advisement. One obvious use of counseling is to encourage students to organize their activities so that their chances of finishing college are improved. In general, guidance can seek to upgrade academic performance and increase options in financial aid, housing, and extracurricular activities which affect students' dropout chances; it can help students become more involved in campus life; and it can point out to them the empirical data regarding the impact on dropout chances of off-campus work and marriage.

Any student, for example, can use the Worksheets to estimate dropout-proneness. For individuals whose dropout chances are high, counselors should consider developing special guidance programs to assist with the environmental obstacles that may cause them to leave college. Counselors or advisers who wish to identify potential dropouts should be alert to certain patterns of behavior strongly related to attrition. Poor academic performance is, of course, one obvious symptom. Less obvious but of substantial importance are two patterns identified in the analyses of work and residence. First, students holding no job or an on-campus job who subsequently take an off-campus job are particularly apt to leave college. The problems are compounded when the off-campus job is also full time. Second, if students who initially enter college as dormitory residents subsequently move out to live with their parents, dropout chances substantially increase. Both these patterns indicate decreasing involvement with campus life. In short, counselors and advisers should look for behavioral or environmental changes that suggest declining commitment to or involvement in the campus community.

Counseling is also helpful to students who wish to transfer from one institution to another. Among junior college students, of course, transferring is necessary to complete the baccalaureate. Since many two-year college students apparently drop out because they are unsuccessful in transferring, counselors in two-year colleges can have a real impact on persistence rates if they can anticipate and reduce the problems inherent in this process. Transferring from one four-year college or university to another is uniformly associated with high dropout rates except in the South; and students who initially enroll at a private four-year college incur an especially high risk of dropping out if they transfer.

One obvious problem is that students who enroll after the freshman year in collegiate institutions with a tradition of yearly classes beginning as freshmen and continuing through graduation are, in effect, interlopers in an existing student culture. The difficulties of socialization and adjustment for the transfer student are apparent. Thus counselors of potential transfer students in four-year institutions would be well advised to encourage them to explore in some depth what they expect of the new institution and perhaps to consider remaining at their present college. And institutions that accept transfer students should develop special programs to facilitate their smooth transition. In particular, incumbent undergraduates should be alerted to the special problems of transfer students and their support enlisted to help integrate these students into the campus culture.

A particularly difficult counseling problem is the leave of absence. Although the word *stopouts* has been applied by some educators to students who take planned leaves of absence, the term as used in this study is somewhat broader, including all students who have had some irregularity in their undergraduate education but who cannot as yet be classified as either dropouts or persisters. By almost all indications, such students resemble dropouts more than persisters. If it were possible to analyze, separately from other stopouts, those students who leave college for a predesignated period with full intention of returning, one might be able to show that the two groups are qualitatively different. In the absence of such information, however, students should be cautioned against leaves of absence. A large number, it seems, do not return to college.

Finally, some institutions are introducing administrative procedures to classify as stopouts those students who formerly would have been called dropouts, in order to simplify their reentry. Although no data from the present study bear directly on such programs, they would seem to maximize the chances that dropouts will return to college.

Financial Aid. Financial aid can be utilized in numerous ways to reduce students' chances of dropping out (see Chapter Three). However, because of the many constraints imposed on state and federal financial aid money (the bulk of the aid to students), institutions have relatively little discretion in awarding such funds. The current federal Basic Educational Opportunity Grant (BEOG), which for the 1974–1975 freshmen represents the most common single source of grant support, is based strictly on an independent determination of student financial need. Many state scholarship programs—the second most likely resource for these freshmen—are similarly outside the control of individual institutions. Perhaps the largest sources of discretionary financial aid for individual institutions are internal funds (such as tuition and endowment income) and funds from the Higher Education Act of 1965: work-study, loans, and grants. Institutions have the responsibility for combining these latter funds to create "packages" of financial aid.

For institutions with some discretionary dollars, several uses can maximize the beneficial impact on student persistence. Where possible, loans should be avoided in favor of other sources, particularly for men. Although grant support is associated with small increases in persistence, it is, of course, an expensive form of aid compared with loans. Work-study programs, universally effective in contributing to greater student persistence, can also be expensive, but there is some return in that useful service is performed by the working student. Work-study appears to have its greatest impact among low-income students when it is *not* combined in a package with grant or loan support.

Institutions should consider financial aid packages cautiously. Modest support from several sources simultaneously is generally associated with somewhat reduced chances of persistence, whereas support from a single source (a loan is the main exception) is generally associated with increased chances of persistence. While the meaning of these findings is not entirely clear, financial aid officers would be well advised to undertake more systematic research on the effects of different amounts and combinations of financial aid.

Work Opportunities. Providing job opportunities for students is one sure way to enhance student persistence. An on-campus job, even during the freshman year, substantially increases the student's chances of finishing college. Federal work-study and other forms of on-campus employment are equally positive in their impact. Whether the job is in an academic or nonacademic sector does not make any appreciable difference, nor does the degree of relevance to the student's course work or career plans. Even job satisfaction is not a major factor; students improve their chances of finishing college even if they dislike their on-campus job. The only qualification concerning positive effects is hours worked; these should be limited to not more than twenty hours per week. Jobs that require more hours not only lose their beneficial impact, but introduce a negative effect that is actually worse than no job at all. In short, institutions should make every effort to increase the number and type of on-campus jobs, but the hours worked should be limited.

Results of off-campus employment can also be positive, although the circumstances must be carefully controlled. Single students who begin college holding a part-time job off-campus generally benefit from such employment in terms of increased chances of completing college. Students who work full time (defined as twenty-five or more hours per week) at off-campus jobs, however, lose any benefit and are actually more likely to drop out than students who hold no jobs. The negative effects of full-time work are greater for off-campus than for on-campus jobs. Further, if a student begins college with no off-campus job and subsequently takes such a job, the prognosis for persistence is poor. It is not entirely clear whether this pattern of no job or on-campus job followed by off-campus employment is a direct cause of dropping out or whether such a shift is a symptom of increasing dropout tendencies. Finally, off-campus employment during the first year of college has negative effects when the student is married at college entry. Apparently, the combined responsibilities of off-campus employment, marriage, and full-time academic work are simply too much for most students. However, federal work-study programs or other on-campus employment is *beneficial* to the student married at college entry.

To push these findings on the positive impact of student employment to the limit, suppose that an institution initiated a long-term program to expand student employment opportunities to the point where there would eventually be part-time jobs on campus for all students who could be persuaded to take them. (Data indicate that, in many institutions, well over half of the student body might be interested in such jobs.) The most likely source of such jobs would be in the numerous nonacademic functions performed by the institution: maintenance, buildings and grounds, clerical work, food service, student bookstore, and so forth. Initially, a few students might be assigned under work-study programs to assist regular employees in carrying out such work. As regular employees retire or resign, they could (where feasible) gradually be replaced by students. After a period of time, many if not most of the nonacademic functions of the institution would either be run by students or rely heavily on student labor.

One likely long-range benefit of such a plan would be economic: the overhead costs of running the institution would probably decline, since part-time student pay would probably amount to less than the salaries of full-time career employees. Other possible effects would be savings in student financial aid and, of course, reductions in dropout rates. Furthermore, sharing directly some of the responsibility for effective operation of the institution (and receiving reasonable compensation at the same time) may well help to develop in the student body a stronger sense of identification with and loyalty to the institution. While some institutions may question the feasibility of such a plan, it should be kept in mind that young people of college age in contrast to many adults are generally able and willing to work for modest pay even at highly menial or repetitive jobs. Perhaps the major difference between students and adults who have to work at these jobs is that students recognize the temporary nature of such employment.

Extracurricular Activities. Although data limitations made possible definitive analyses of only two extracurricular activities, the student's chances of staying in college seem to be enhanced by involvement in them. The two activities studied—membership in social fraternities or sororities and participation in varsity athletics —seem to increase persistence rates among both men and women, as well as blacks and whites. The one exception is participation in varsity athletics by blacks attending black colleges; conceivably, intense athletic competition at some colleges is a mitigating factor here.

To capitalize on such findings, institutions should increase opportunities for extracurricular activities, facilitate student entry into such activities, and encourage students to take part. Expanding such activities is especially important in the large institutions, where there are many activities but the likelihood of participation in certain areas (student government, for instance) is reduced because of limits on the number of participants. When it is not feasible to enlarge the number of participants in a given activity—varsity athletics, for example—it might be possible to expand or initiate parallel activities, such as intramural athletics.

Housing and Student Services. Living in a dormitory during the freshman year increases the student's chances of finishing college. These positive effects exist for men and women, for blacks and whites, and in nearly every type of institution (the single exception is the public two-year college, and in this case the sample may have been too small or otherwise unrepresentative).

Though institutions are usually not in a position to undertake the independent construction of new residential facilities, every effort should be made to fill existing housing. Those colleges with underutilized residences can attract more students to live on campus by reducing costs, improving facilities and programming, or instituting required campus residence.

The benefits of dormitory living are not lost through a residence requirement (see Chapter Five). Many institutions, however, have dropped such requirements and others on occasion have been subjected to legal action by students who want them removed. While the creation of a residence requirement raises certain ethical and legal issues beyond the scope of this study, students can be encouraged to live in dormitories in numerous ways short of a requirement: counseling, orientation, special application materials, and physical improvements to the facilities.

Living in sorority or fraternity houses during the freshman or sophomore years increases students' chances of persistence in much the same way as dormitory living. Although the popularity of sororities and fraternities declined somewhat during the 1960s, many such organizations have survived by liberalizing their admissions policies and, in some cases, by converting their houses into dormitory-like facilities where almost any student who can pay the cost is permitted to live.

Living away from home in a private room or apartment appears to increase a man's chances of finishing college, but not as much as living in a dormitory. For women, however, dropout chances are generally increased by living in a private room or apartment. Favoring women over men in allocating residential facilities may be justified, particularly if the woman applicant unable to find a place in a dormitory will be forced to live in a private room or apartment.

Many institutions give priority to students who come from long distances in allocating available residential facilities. Their justification is usually economic: presumably, students who live in the same town as the college can live at home if they wish. Such practices are highly questionable, particularly with undergraduate men. The man who must live away from home because of distance can still increase his chances of finishing college by living in a private room or apartment. However, if the local student is denied a place in a residence hall on the ground that he or she can just as well live at home, the likelihood that the student will choose instead a private room or apartment is probably somewhat reduced. The economic reasoning behind favoring students who come a long distance is inconsistent with the educational consequences for local students. If local students are not to be favored, then a policy of nondiscrimination in relation to distance from home seems the most equitable and also the easiest to justify in terms of likely educational outcomes.

Because of the apparent value of living in a residence hall on campus, institutions with such facilities might want to study ways to enhance the normal positive effect of residential living. Such studies should include an assessment of the effects of roommates, peer groups, living-study arrangements in the residence halls, programming, and staffing of facilities. The results might well put institutions in a position to capitalize still more on the potential value of the residence hall experience.

Commuter colleges and colleges that cannot accommodate all students in existing residence halls need not necessarily view the data on the impact of residence as irrelevant. Indeed, these data should challenge the colleges' ingenuity and resourcefulness. Commuter institutions might devise approaches to *simulate* the residential experience so students would spend more time on campus and interact more. If the theory about involvement and persistence is valid (and many findings support it), any programs that involve the commuter student in campus life and activities presumably will have a positive effect on persistence. If nothing else, institutions should experiment with such techniques on selected students.

Two-Year Colleges. The relatively high dropout rate among students at community colleges who plan to earn a bachelor's degree results from several factors: the high dropout-proneness of entering students, the lack of both financial aid and job opportunities on campus, and the absence of student housing. Even when these factors are considered, two-year institutions have somewhat higher dropout rates than expected. The most likely explanation for this finding lies in the transfer process.

Leaders in the community college movement have long recognized the importance of transfer for those students who aspire to a baccalaureate or higher degree. No matter how sophisticated the junior college's approach to this process, one would expect a certain loss of students simply from the physical move and the paper work involved. The incumbent undergraduate in a four-year institution only has to show up each year at the same place and at approximately the same time to complete his or her undergraduate education. An initial point of attack for the two-year colleges, therefore, is the mechanics of transferring. It is difficult to overestimate the importance of adequate guidance, record keeping, and communications in helping students to make the transition smoothly. For useful suggestions on how to enhance student persistence in community colleges, see Brawer (1973) and MacMillan (1970).

Two-year institutions, of course, are more or less at the mercy of the recipient institution in their attempts to ease the transfer for academically oriented undergraduates. No matter how efficiently the two-year institution handles its part, any potential transfer students can become discouraged by inefficiency or any sign of reluctance on the part of upper-division institutions. Given their increasing interest in these students as a means to keep enrollments up, however, these institutions should do everything they can to attract and enroll the largest possible number of qualified transfers. In this sense, then, the recipient institution has an equal stake in smoothing the shift. The two-year colleges and recipient upper-division institutions might well profit from joint meetings to work out the logistical details.

Educational Policy

Educational policy-makers include legislators in municipal, state, and federal governments, top-level administrators in the executive branches of these governments, and advisors to the legislative and executive branches. A relatively new but increasingly important group of policy-making bodies comprises the councils and boards that govern or coordinate *systems* of institutions in cities and states. Some of these agencies merely coordinate the activities of the institutions for which they are responsible, whereas others actually set policy. To improve the effectiveness and efficiency of institutions located within a particular geographic region is the common concern of almost all educational policy-makers. Numerous findings from this study relate to matters over which educational policy-makers have some control, such as financial aid, tuition, admissions, facilities construction, development of new institutions, and coordination and evaluation of institutions within a system.

Financial Aid. Most undergraduate financial aid comes from public funds appropriated by city, state, and federal legislatures.

The purpose is basically twofold: to permit more students to attend college and to enable them to earn the degree. The latter aspect is the focus here.

Certainly the most clear-cut finding is the positive impact of student employment on persistence. Participation in federal work-study programs, as well as other on-campus work, benefits both men and women, as well as blacks and whites (the impact is especially pronounced among blacks at both black and white colleges). Persistence rates are also increased by other forms of on-campus employment. While grants also appear to increase the student's chances of completing college, the effects are generally smaller than for work. Depending on the third major category of financial aid—repayable loans—appears to *decrease* the man's chances of completing college; results for women are inconclusive.

Those who set financial aid policy and determine how resources will be allocated face certain dilemmas. Assuming that they will eventually be repaid, loans represent a relatively inexpensive source of aid, but they are apparently the least effective in enabling students to complete college (indeed, men appear better off with no aid than with loans). Student employment is the most effective way to maximize persistence, a finding which reinforces the notion that any program that involves the student actively in the campus life decreases attrition. Policy-makers who might push for a greater investment of financial aid in expanding student work opportunities should keep in mind these qualifications: first, the place of work. Jobs on-campus are clearly superior to off-campus employment, although off-campus employment can be effective if the student is not married, if the work is less than full time, and if the off-campus job becomes part of the student's established pattern of activities during the freshman year. Second, the number of hours worked. More than twenty hours a week, particularly for women, not only eliminates the beneficial effects of jobs, but also reverses the effects to the point where the student is better off not working at all.

Caution should be exercised in developing financial aid packages. Students who depend on more than one source of aid during the freshman year have increased chances of dropping out compared with students who depend heavily on a single source such as grants. In a sense, then, such sources as work-study or grants lose their effectiveness if they are provided in relatively small amounts to make up a total package of aid. Complex interactions among the variables—type and amount of financial aid, need, and college costs—make it difficult to say whether there are ways that various types of aid can be packaged so as to enhance rather than inhibit the student's chances of finishing college. Considering the complexity of the problem and the large sums involved, policy-makers might consider allocating a fraction of such aid to systematic research on these interacting factors. Such research would almost surely provide a better empirical basis for developing future policies.

Tuition. The national debate about tuition involves several issues outside the scope of this study: competition between public and private higher education, increased access for economically disadvantaged students, and the question of who should pay the bills. This study provides some evidence, however, on a related matter—whether persistence, particularly among students from low-income families, is affected by the cost of the college.

Clearly, the data do not show that moderate or high tuition is an obstacle to completing college, except for blacks attending black colleges, where relatively high tuition *does* appear to have a negative effect on persistence. In fact, persistence is poorest for both men and women at the low-cost colleges and, among men, greatest at the high-cost colleges. (Women persist equally well in moderate- and high-cost colleges.) This negative impact of low-tuition colleges occurs primarily because most two-year colleges—which have poor holding power on students—have low tuitions.

When the effect of tuition is considered in terms of the income level of students' parents, the results are different. Among students from low-income families high tuition is positively related to persistence for men and negatively for women—possibly because men from low-income families who attend high-cost colleges get larger scholarship stipends than low-income women attending these same colleges. But the inconclusive and complex nature of these findings underscores the need for further study of the relationships among college costs, financial need, financial aid, sex, and student attrition.

Admissions. How students should be admitted to campuses within a multiinstitutional public system has become a highly controversial topic. Some elite and well-known public institutions, such as the City University of New York, which have based their selective admissions policies on the traditional measures of high school grades and test scores, have been forced to modify these policies to admit students across a wider range of ability and preparation. Other hierarchical systems (for example, the three-tier California system) have maintained their traditional patterns of differential selectivity.

Planners and policy-makers responsible for multiinstitutional systems are interested in how the differential selectivity of institutions within the system affects the students. Is a hierarchical arrangement superior to a homogeneous institutional arrangement? What are the consequences for bright students? For average or below-average students?

A hierarchical system may *not* be the most efficacious in maximizing student persistence. The greatest difficulty appears to be the low selectivity of the open-door institutions (normally the two-year or community colleges). Students who attend such institutions aspiring to bachelor's or higher degrees appear to be penalized by increased dropout chances. These effects apply to the few bright students who end up in such institutions, as well as to the average and below-average students. Obstacles to persistence are numerous. Most obvious are the absence of residential facilities, limited job opportunities, and problems of commuting; more subtle are lack of a collegiate community and difficulties in transferring to a four-year institution.

At the top of the hierarchy, the few average students who gain admission to the most selective institutions do *not* experience any greater difficulty than comparable students attending moderately selective institutions. If anything, the average student's chances of finishing are slightly better at the more selective campus.

Perhaps the most important conclusion is that, except for the negative effects of the two-year institutions on persistence, there is no support for the widely held belief that only the brightest students *should* attend the more selective institutions or that bright students are penalized if they are forced to attend an institution further down in the hierarchy. If anything, students of all ability levels have the best chance of finishing college when they attend a moderately selective institution.

Clearly, in a hierarchical system in which two-year colleges occupy the lowest level, admission to this tier does not represent an "equal educational opportunity" for bachelor's degree aspirants compared with admission to institutions on higher tiers. Chances of completing college are substantially less in the two-year colleges, particularly because residential facilities are absent. Under traditional selective admissions policies, the highest achieving students are allowed access to *any* level of the system (a pure tracking system would deny such students admittance to the least selective colleges). The lowest achieving students, however, are barred from all but the lowest tier. The rationale for such differential admissions, never clearly stated, is not supported by this study.

Although supporters use the importance of diversity as a justification for hierarchical systems, institutional variety can be achieved in other ways. One major alternative to a hierarchical or vertical system is a horizontal form, where institutions differ not so much in prestige (student ability, faculty salaries, research productivity, expenditures, and so forth), but in *curricular* emphases or pedagogical styles. The possibilities for diversity here are almost limitless.

Given these empirical findings and possible institutional alternatives, educational policy-makers could initiate systemwide investigations of the advantages and disadvantages of alternative structures. Even if such studies do not result in the alteration of existing structures, they may at least provide a more comprehensive rationale for existing systems than is now available.

Facilities Construction. Since living on campus in a student residence increases a student's chances of completing college, policymakers might reexamine current trends toward withdrawing support for construction of residential facilities. Decisions of this type, of course, are necessarily complex and involve many considerations other than reducing dropout rates. Nevertheless, for those systems where additional residential facilities are a viable option, these findings provide support for that choice.

Some benefits of residential living derive from geographic

factors: students must necessarily leave home and be closely exposed to other students and to the campus environment in general. Most commuters do not have similar opportunities for close exposure to peers and for participation in campus life. Commuting can also be an expensive, frustrating, and time-consuming experience. Aside from these obvious effects, however, the positive impact of residence halls is poorly understood in terms of the *mechanisms* of influence. What architectural arrangements are most likely to maximize the benefits of dormitory living? Where should these buildings be located in relation to other campus facilities? What about the value of coeducational dormitories? Should residences be designed like motels or should common living areas be arranged to maximize student contact? Are live-in facilities for faculty members of any value? If research on existing variations in architecture were carried out systematically, the results could provide a basis for future design and construction. Considering the large cost of construction, the relatively small cost of research could yield substantial benefits.

New Institutions. Although the 1970s are witnessing a tapering off of the rapid development in the 1960s of new college campuses, many public systems of higher education will continue to add campuses during the next ten or fifteen years. Although the complex problem of designing new campuses in a public system is far beyond this study, certain issues should be confronted in developing new institutions.

The difficulties of two-year colleges and commuter colleges in general have been mentioned. If the primary purpose of a new campus is to provide four-year undergraduate education (rather than vocational or technical education or some alternative postsecondary form not leading to a bachelor's degree), then the efficacy of adding more traditionally designed community colleges is questionable. Of the various public institutions in this study, the four-year undergraduate college is the best model in terms of costs and benefits. While the costs are certainly less than those of the traditional research university, the student's chances of completing his or her undergraduate education in the four-year college are actually greater than in the public university. Although the particular features that contribute to the effectiveness of these institutions are not completely understood, among the more critical are an emphasis on undergraduates rather than graduate education, available residential facilities, a heterogeneous student body, diverse curricular offerings, and a collegiate environment.

The pressure to build more commuter institutions, whether two- or four-year, presents a dilemma to the educational planner and policy-maker. Commuter institutions presumably provide relatively low-cost, easy-access higher education for residents in a particular geographic region. Members of the community can attend these colleges for relatively little money and with relatively little interference in their everyday activities. Student convenience is further enhanced because many institutions schedule classes during the late afternoon and evening hours, an arrangement that permits people to hold full-time jobs and also attend college full time.

But one pays a certain price for such easy access to post-secondary education. By minimizing the disruption in the student's outside life, involvement in the educational process is likewise decreased. Students merely have to show up on campus for an hour or so to attend classes and find some time at home to complete assignments and study for examinations. There are no peers to interact with during meals or in the evening, no encouragement to participate in extracurricular activities, and often no campus of the type found at residential institutions. Indeed, the commuter, in contrast to the resident, interacts less with faculty and students and participates in fewer academic and social activities at the institution (Chickering, 1974).

This reduction in the socializing effects of the traditional collegiate experience is perhaps of minor importance to many nontraditional students: those who are married, older, or attending part time. (This study is limited to full-time students.) However, for the traditional student—the eighteen-year-old who has just completed high school and is pursuing a baccalaureate on a full-time basis—being deprived of a collegiate experience and attending a commuter institution are clearly not the ideal undergraduate education. In short, educational planners developing new institutions to serve these students should consider alternatives to the typical commuter college. Although the costs of traditional residential institutions are probably much greater than those of traditional community colleges, the benefits in terms of increased student persistence are also much higher.

Higher education for nontraditional students can be expanded with models other than the traditional commuter college, such as Empire State College of the State University of New York. A team visiting Empire State for the regional accrediting association (Middle States Accrediting Association, 1974) suggested that it *is* possible to obtain a high degree of involvement and commitment even among older students who simultaneously hold full-time jobs. While the efficacy of these nontraditional forms compared with traditional commuter colleges has not been explored empirically, anecdotal evidence from the accrediting team suggests that these forms merit careful consideration as alternatives.

Multiinstitutional Systems. Most multiinstitutional systems involve two- as well as four-year institutions. To maximize student persistence rates, articulation between the two- and four-year segments of these systems clearly has top priority. Since many students who attend two-year institutions subsequently transfer to private institutions, articulation between these two groups is also needed. While two-year institutions must improve communications with four-year private institutions about the transfer process, the latter group might also regard such improvement as in its own interest to keep enrollments up.

Students who transfer from four-year institutions present certain problems. Except in the southern states, these students have substantially reduced chances of persisting at their second institution. One obvious problem is that students who enroll after the freshman year are, in effect, interlopers in an existing student culture, particularly in collegiate institutions where a "class" begins as freshmen and continues through graduation. The difficulties in socialization for the transfer student are apparent. Four-year institutions should be encouraged by coordinating agencies to develop special programs to assist transfer students make a smooth transition. Incumbent undergraduates should be alerted to the special problems of the transfer student and their support should be enlisted to help integrate these students into the campus culture.

Evaluating Institutions Within a System. Many educational policy-makers are interested in evaluating the comparative performance of different institutions within the system. Although systemwide evaluation has traditionally been done on a cost basis (through examining relative institutional expenditures for salaries, facilities, libraries, and so forth), planners have become increasingly sophisticated about the need for cost-benefit analyses in which some measures of institutional productivity or output are utilized. Clearly, several principles should be followed in developing any comparative analysis of institutional outputs.

1. A simple output measure based on degrees granted or credit hours awarded can be misleading, since institutions vary widely in the percentage of students who actually seek to complete an undergraduate degree. In this sense, then, degrees and credits must be assessed in relation to the number of students who initially pursue them.

2. Even if this relative assessment is made, the results can be misleading, given the diversity among institutions in the dropout-proneness of their initial recruits. Under these circumstances, rates of graduation or degree completion can be evaluated only in relation to the rates that would be *expected,* given students' abilities, aspirations, past achievements, and social background.

3. Even with adjustments for initial student dropout-proneness, an institution's relative dropout rate may be higher than expected because it lacks certain resources such as residential facilities and job and financial aid opportunities, or lower than expected because it has these resources in abundance.

4. As a general principle of evaluation, policy-makers should seek *explanations* for the differential attrition rates of different institutions, rather than simply determining whether the rates are above or below expectation. Only by understanding the underlying causes of deviations can policy-makers replicate the successes of institutions performing above expectation and avoid repeating the nonproductive practices of those performing below expectation. An ongoing program of evaluative research is necessary, in which the flow of students through all institutions within a system is examined over time and in which various institutional practices and procedures are documented.

Resource Allocation. While the political and practical complexities of budgeting for multiinstitutional systems make it difficult to formulate specific proposals for any particular system, the results of this study point to several areas where increased financial support is likely to increase student persistence. These would include providing on-campus employment for students, improving or expanding residential facilities, strengthening orientation programs for new students and counseling programs directed at transfer students, and supporting multicampus research and evaluation (see the final section of this chapter for specific suggestions concerning possible research projects).

Implications for Students

Prospective college students can use a number of these findings to increase their chances of completing college, with three qualifications. First, the results apply primarily to single students who are recent high school graduates. Second, since the results were obtained only with students who began college on a full-time basis, many generalizations probably do not apply to the part-time student. And third, the findings are probably not applicable to students who are not pursuing a degree or are pursuing only an associate degree.

This summary of implications for students follows the pattern of the earlier chapters on predicting dropout chances, financial aid, work, residence, and type of college. A final section deals with special problems confronting married students.

Predicting Dropout Chances. To estimate their chances of dropping out, students should answer the questions in the Worksheets and follow the instructions for computing their dropout probabilities. Two probabilities can be computed. The first uses only data about the student; the second, more elaborate prediction utilizes data not only about the student but also about financial aid, work, and residence. These probabilities, of course, are merely *estimates;* each student's unique situation may substantially alter the estimate. The student, counselor, and parents are the best judges of these extraneous factors.

Financial Aid and Work. Students should obtain an on-campus job, if possible, during their freshman year. The main qualification for this job is that the number of hours should be kept down (preferably not over twenty hours per week). Having a job is particularly important for black students, whether they attend black or white colleges.

If possible, students (particularly men) should avoid loans, seeking alternative means of support. Even an off-campus job, provided it is not full time, is preferable to borrowing. The one exception is married students, who should probably avoid off-campus work during the freshman year.

Scholarships and grants, of course, are desirable sources of aid because they usually come with no strings attached. In addition, a scholarship or grant will probably increase slightly the student's chances of completing college (but not as much as having a job).

Residence. Both men and women should, where possible, find a place in a college dormitory. Even if this means attending an institution different from the student's first choice, the benefit may be worth the extra effort. If dormitory facilities are unavailable, men still benefit in terms of reduced dropout probabilities by living away from home in a private room or apartment. For women who cannot find a dormitory space, however, living away from home in a private room or apartment adds substantially to the chances of dropping out. Freshmen women, it would appear, find it more difficult to adapt to off-campus private living than do freshmen men.

Students tempted by the independence that goes with living in a private room or apartment are reminded that this preference is typical: a large proportion of the freshmen entering college in the fall of 1974 (Astin, King, Light, and Richardson, 1974) said they would rather live in a private room than at home or in a dormitory. In spite of these preferences, students' chances of finishing college are greater if they live in dormitories or in fraternity or sorority houses.

Students who must live with their parents during the first year of college substantially boost their chances of staying in college if they move into a dormitory or fraternity or sorority house during their sophomore year. Thus, even if finances or lack of facilities prevent the student from living in a dormitory as a freshman, efforts to do so during subsequent years are generally rewarded with increased chances of finishing college.

Choosing a College. The probability that a student will obtain the degree can be significantly affected by the type of institution selected. Students maximize their chances by attending a private university in any region or a public four-year college located in the Northeastern or Southern states. Their chances are minimal if they attend a two-year institution, regardless of region. Attending either a Roman Catholic or Protestant institution also increases the probability of finishing college. This effect is particularly great when the student's own religious orientation corresponds to that of the institution; however, for a male student from a Jewish family or a family with no religious affiliation, the beneficial effects of a sectarian institution are substantially reduced.

Contrary to popular belief, attending a highly selective institution does not increase the student's chances of dropping out. Indeed, students are likeliest to persist if they go to moderately selective institutions. Institutions of low selectivity, including most junior colleges, appear to increase the likelihood of dropping out. Students of moderate ability should not avoid highly selective institutions for fear of jeopardizing their chances of finishing. At the same time, highly able students should not avoid moderately selective institutions on the grounds that they will become bored or otherwise disenchanted. (These recommendations, of course, are based *solely* on the impact of institutional selectivity on persistence; other considerations, such as costs and the value of a degree from a particular institution, should also enter into a student's choice of college.)

Except for small institutions (fewer than 500 students)', which appear to increase dropout chances, size of institution makes little difference, although students from farms or small-town backgrounds are more likely to drop out of a large institution (over 20,000 students). At the same time, the negative effects of attending a small institution (enrollment below 500) appear exaggerated if the student is from an urban or suburban background.

Overall, tuition costs, as such, appear to have no strong relationship to dropping out. However, among students from families in the lower income brackets, women have a little less chance of completing college when the costs are high, while men have a slightly *increased* chance.

Black students who wish to attend predominantly white institutions should remember that their chances of completing college will be somewhat less than they would be at a black college, based on the data from this study. But because the racial climate in predominantly white institutions today is probably better than when these data were collected in 1968–1972, the difference may not be as great.

Academic Performance. No matter what the student's grades in high school or what the scores on admissions tests, college grades will have a major bearing on whether or not the student completes his or her undergraduate work. Factors that enhance both grades and persistence are participation in honors programs and credit by examination. Persistence is also enhanced if the student studies abroad, but travel abroad without formal study should be avoided.

Extracurricular Activities. Because of data limitations, it was possible to study participation in only two extracurricular activities: varsity sports and social fraternities or sororities. Both activities enhance the student's chances of finishing college.

Marriage. Evidence is substantial that the effects of residence, work, and financial aid are different for married and single students. Married students just starting college should avoid off-campus work and, if they need a job, make every effort to get one on campus. Full-time work should also be avoided, on or off campus.

If possible, married undergraduates should be able to count on their spouse for a major part of their college costs. Whatever the arrangement, it should be clear-cut from the beginning; ambivalent or inconsistent support from the spouse is a poor prognostic sign. For students who contemplate marriage while still enrolled, support from the spouse is also an important positive factor.

Women should keep in mind that marriage usually has a vastly different effect on their chances of completing college compared with those of their husbands. Thus, being married at college entry or getting married while still enrolled substantially decreases the likelihood that the woman will gain the degree, whereas men actually persist better if they are married when they enter or get married before finishing college. Having children, on the other hand, substantially reduces the chances of finishing college for both sexes, especially women.

Dropping out tends to push men and women into traditional sex roles. Practically all married men dropouts work full-time. Among the married women dropouts, unemployment or part-time employment is much more common than among married women who finish college.

Summary. The pattern of choices that maximizes the student's chances of finishing college comprises attendance at either a private university or a public four-year college, living on campus in a dormitory or fraternity or sorority house, a part-time job on campus, scholarship or grant support, membership in campus organizations or participation in extracurricular activities, deferring marriage, and the best grades possible.

Overview of Findings

By combining the predictive factors reported in Chapters Two through Seven, one can obtain a composite picture of the personal and environmental factors that maximize a student's chances of finishing college. The most important entering characteristics are the student's high school grades, degree aspirations, and religious background: students with good grades, plans for postgraduate degrees, Jewish parents, and Jewish religious preferences have the best chance of finishing college; those with poor grades, plans for only a bachelor's or "other" degree, Protestant parents, and no religious preference have the poorest chance. (For black students, being a cigarette smoker is also among the strongest predictors of dropping out.) The entering characteristics next in importance for staying in college are having good study habits, having high expectations about academic performance in college, having highly educated parents, being married (for men), and being single (for women). Other entering characteristics that add significantly but less powerfully to college persistence are high scores on college admissions tests, being Oriental, being a nonsmoker, and growing up in a moderate-size city or town.

After these entering characteristics are taken into account, the student's chances of finishing college can be improved by a number of experiential factors. By far the most important of these is getting good grades in college. Next in importance are staying single (for women) and not having children (both sexes), living in a college dormitory rather than at home, and having a part-time job (full-time jobs are to be avoided). Persistence is also enhanced by participation in ROTC or in extracurricular activities such as sports and fraternities or sororities. Being supported by one's parents also helps, as does having a scholarship or grant, but loans add little, and, for men, they reduce chances of finishing college. Students who transfer from one four-year college to another also have somewhat reduced persistence chances.

When the student's entering characteristics, place of residence, financial aid, and work status are taken into account, the college attended can still exert an influence. Chances are maximized by attending a private university in any region or a public four-year college in the northeastern or southern states, and they are minimized by attending a public two-year college. Chances are also improved by attendance at a moderately selective (rather than a highly selective or nonselective) college or a religiously affiliated college.

The degree of fit between the student and the college can also affect persistence. Basically, students' chances are improved if their backgrounds are similar to those of other students: Students persist better at religious colleges if their own religious background is similar; blacks persist better at black colleges than at white colleges; and students from small towns persist better in small colleges. Contrary to popular belief, however, students do not necessarily progress better if they attend colleges with students of similar ability.

Implications for Research

The numerous empirical results of this study suggest promising directions for future research. Possible topics and projects are described briefly under the following headings: A Theory of College Persistence, Student Predictors of Dropping Out, Financial Aid and Work, Residence, Academic Factors, and Institutional Factors.

Theory of College Persistence. This study supports the theory that student involvement is a key factor in persistence. Briefly, this theory holds that a student's tendency to drop out of college is inversely related to the degree of direct involvement in the academic and social life of the institution. Backing this notion are the positive effects on persistence of participation in extracurricular activities, work-study and other on-campus employment, participation in ROTC and honors programs, and dormitory living. The strong relationship between academic performance and persistence is also, in a sense, additional support for this theory, given the assumption that getting good grades is a sign of student involvement in the academic life and environment of the institution.

Possible future research in this area might include developing independent psychological measures of student involvement. If the theory is correct, such measures should be highly predictive of dropout behavior and should, at the same time, correlate substantially with behavioral measures in this study. Related research could identify other behavioral measures (through direct observations of students on campus, in dormitories, in classrooms, and so forth) that might also indicate involvement. An interesting aspect of this theory concerns individual differences among students. Certain students (high-ability students, black students, men versus women, and so forth) might manifest their involvement in different ways.

The possible therapeutic value of dropping out is another important subject for research. Although this study identified means to keep students in college, undoubtedly in many instances they actually benefit from dropping out. The problem is how to separate these students from those for whom it has undesirable consequences. Unfortunately, the prevailing tendency today is to rationalize dropping out by suggesting in a deterministic fashion that dropouts are really better off out of college after all. The challenge for researchers is to develop operational ways to separate the "good" from the "bad" dropouts. Presumably, these two groups would not show the same patterns of antecedent causal factors. More important, the ability to distinguish between them would provide a framework for research on remedial procedures to reduce dropping out among students who should not leave college.

Student Predictors. An intriguing set of findings from the predictive analysis in Chapter Two concerns study habits. While many predictive items were consistent with popular notions of good and poor study habits, several produced somewhat unexpected findings, such as the negative relationships of persistence with work for extra credit or keeping a neat study place, and the positive relationship with making careless mistakes on tests. Further research into these and related items measuring student study habits might provide clues to possible remedial efforts.

The contrasting findings for men and women who marry present an opportunity to research sex roles and college persistence. One question should be whether the effects of marriage on persistence are similar for men and women whose sex roles are less differentiated along traditional lines.

Perhaps the most interesting predictor of all was smoking behavior, which had a strong negative association with persistence among white students and an even stronger one among black students. The relationships among smoking, academic performance, and college persistence are fertile ground for future interdisciplinary research focusing on physiological as well as psychological and behavioral variables.

Financial Aid and Work. This study raises as many issues of financial policy as it settles. Although it supports policies that emphasize work-study and grants rather than loans, many questions remain unanswered. Why should a given form of financial aid appear to have less impact when combined with other forms of aid? Why do loans have a negative effect on persistence among men and no effect among women? Why should "minor" support from loans and grants, under certain conditions, be worse than no support at all? What forms of packaging are most efficacious in enhancing student persistence? How important is the amount of a particular form of aid? What are the interactions among type and amount of aid, packaging, parental income, sex, and college costs? All these factors interact in highly complex ways.

A note of caution about future studies of financial aid: short of true experimentation with various forms and combinations, any correlational studies should, at a minimum, exert multivariate controls over the following biasing variables: student ability, aspirations, race, sex, and social background; marital status; parental or family income; student concern about finances; residence while attending college (dormitory, private room, or parents' home); type of job held (if any) and hours worked; and type of college. At a minimum, controls over college type should include measures of level (two-year, four-year, university), control (public, private nonsectarian, Protestant, Catholic), selectivity, sex (coeducational or single sex) and race (predominantly black versus predominantly white). Without such controls the possibility of finding spurious effects of particular forms of financial aid is substantial.

Residence. The benefits of dormitory and fraternity or sorority living offer numerous avenues for research. What parts of the residential experience encourage students to stay in college? How important is the architecture of the residence hall? What are the effects of different types of roommate assignments? How important is staffing? What about programming for dormitory residents? Is the location of the dormitory on campus important? What are the effects of coeducational dormitories and their variations (such as alternate floors versus alternate rooms)? Given greater dormitory demand than supply, which students are most likely to benefit from dormitory living? Why should living in a private room have positive effects for freshman men and negative effects for freshman women? These and related questions offer attractive possibilities for research in which alternative methods of selecting students, programming dormitories, and making roommate assignments are tried.

For institutions with no residential facilities, the positive effects of dormitory living offer challenges for student services. Is it possible to simulate the residential experience in a nonresidential institution? Can existing facilities be utilized to encourage greater interaction among students and between students and faculty? Can commuting students be involved more actively in campus activities?

Academic Factors. The student's academic performance has a direct effect on the decision to remain in or leave college, independent of past ability and achievement. Therefore, it might be possible to control dropout behavior by experimental manipulation of grades. Would such manipulation actually result in greater student involvement and, ultimately, greater achievement? Is it possible that poorly performing students can be motivated eventually to improve their academic performance by controlling the type of evaluative feedback they receive? Can achievement be enhanced through the use of alternative grading systems? What is the impact of putting students on probation?

A related area is the positive impact of honors programs. Are the grades awarded in such programs simply higher, or do students actually achieve more with special attention? Is it possible to increase the number of students participating in honors programs without diluting the effect? Could honors programs be developed separately within curricular areas, thereby giving students a greater opportunity to demonstrate particular talents? These could be hypotheses for experimental research on the relationships among special programs, academic performance, and persistence.

Another avenue of research is suggested by the positive association between credit by examination and persistence. How does this effect operate? Is accelerated progress the principal factor, or are students motivated by the knowledge that they will not have to take courses in subject areas in which they are already competent? Experimental studies on credit by examination, administered on a comprehensive level, could be informative. How important is student boredom in affecting academic performance and, ultimately, the decision to drop out? How does one assess boredom empirically? Can boredom be reduced through better course selection, counseling, or inservice training of teachers?

Institutional Factors. The contrasting effects of public two- and four-year colleges suggest additional research into environmental differences between the two. How important is the collegiate atmosphere (presumably more prevalent at the four-year college)? What role do residential facilities play? How important is peer group influence? Does the presence of many students who are vocationally oriented or who are not pursuing baccalaureate degrees have an adverse affect on students who seek the baccalaureate?

About the problems of transfer for the community college student: What are the obstacles to such a transition? How important are the bureaucratic procedures, such as application forms, letters of acceptance, and so forth? Can these procedures be streamlined and the number of dropouts thereby reduced? Here again, the possibilities for experimental research within public systems are intriguing. Certain procedures could be tried in selected institutions, or contrasting remedial approaches could be tried and compared simultaneously.

A variety of studies are possible on student-institutional

"fit." Why do black students drop out more frequently when they attend predominantly white institutions? Why do students from farms and rural backgrounds seem to drop out more frequently if they enter large institutions? Why are students with Jewish or with no religious background frequently likely to leave traditionally sectarian institutions?

Institutional Research. The foregoing paragraphs make a number of suggestions suitable for institutional self-study. The unique problems of research at a single college, however, merit special attention. The major limitation of such research is the absence of data on comparable institutions that could provide a broad context within which the institution could view its own data. (Institutions can and do participate in multiinstitutional consortia in order to obtain such comparative data, but for purposes of this discussion we shall consider research possibilities that do not require such data.)

One obvious requirement for meaningful institutional research on the dropout question is an adequate data base, including data on each entering freshman class and the capacity to collect follow-up data on each student. Results of the current study (see in particular the Worksheets) also suggest that adequate prediction of persistence and attrition requires a wide range of data. Institutions do not have to limit themselves to the items used in this national study. Indeed, the results of the current study suggest a number of areas (study habits, smoking) where the inclusion of additional items in a freshman questionnaire might substantially improve both predictive accuracy and understanding of the dropout phenomenon.

Follow-ups should include information not only about the student's academic and career progress, but also about the student's experiences since entering college. Here again is an opportunity to elaborate on areas of experience that appeared critical to college persistence in the current study (place of residence, work status, and financial aid packages). In large institutions, it is also important to include in the follow-up information on the particular curricular or social subgroup to which the student belonged. These subgroups are in certain respects analogous to institutions in the current study.

Another possible refinement of the current study is to include more questions on students' reasons for dropping out. Such data can provide clues to possible causal factors, although it is naive to assume that these reasons adequately explain why a given student leaves college. Each dropout should not have to pick a single reason from a list since the decision to leave college is likely to depend on a number of considerations (in the current study, for example, dropouts picked an average of two reasons from the list, even though they were limited to a maximum of three). One alternative is to ask students to indicate the degree of importance of each possible reason and at the same time to permit (but not require) them to select one as most important.

Students' reasons for dropping out are perhaps most useful in classifying students for purposes of analyzing antecedent factors in a longitudinal study. It may turn out, for example, that entering student and environmental variables which predict dropping out for academic reasons are quite different from the variables which predict dropping out because of marriage or children. Such analysis requires large samples, but a possible refinement is to do follow-up interviews with dropouts in order to test in depth, on an anecdotal level, the validity of students' reasons as reported in a survey instrument. Such interviews might provide important clues as to how such "explanations" should be worded in future surveys.

These recommendations for longitudinal institutional research will clearly take time to implement in those institutions that currently have no data base. One quick alternative for such institutions is to collect data from their next entering class and to compute expected dropout rates using the formulas in the Worksheets. Rates could be computed for the institution as a whole as well as for subunits (schools, colleges, departments). These expected rates could then be compared with actual rates from earlier entering classes to obtain preliminary estimates both of overall holding power and of the relative holding power of various units within the institution. These initial freshman data could eventually become the basis for long-term longitudinal studies.

Summary. These suggestions do not by any means exhaust the possibilities for practical research. Researchers are urged to read the particular chapters for more detailed suggestions. Although in many cases experimentation is to be preferred over correlational research, such as the current study, various constraints may prevent such experimentation. Under these circumstances, investigators who opt for nonexperimental or correlational studies should keep in mind the many biasing variables to be controlled. At a minimum, they should simultaneously collect longitudinal data from students attending several institutions and apply multivariate controls to student variables, as well as to measures of financial aid, work status, place of residence, and type of institution. They should be alerted to the possible need to adjust for errors in measurement of characteristics of entering students (for a full discussion of this highly technical problem, see Astin, 1975).

WORKSHEETS FOR PREDICTING CHANCES OF DROPPING OUT

This section will enable policy-makers, administrators, and students to compute measures of dropout-proneness for any individual student or any group of students. Individual students can simply answer the questions in the attached tables and compute their own probabilities of dropping out. The probabilities are based on the predictions in which stopouts and dropouts were combined. Average measures of dropout-proneness for any group of students can also be calculated directly from aggregate student data, assuming appropriate data are available. In using such data, the mean values can be treated in exactly the same way as an individual student's response to a particular question. The procedures for using the tables are as follows:

Step 1. Answer each question and record the score associated with that answer in the space provided. If the answer is not available for a particular question, substitute the mean value from the appropriate student group (white men, white women, blacks in black colleges, or blacks in white colleges). In certain circumstances it may make more sense to estimate the response rather than to use the mean. For example, for a student at a highly selective college who does not report his or her average high school grades, it may be more appropriate to substitute the mean grades for students at that college (if available) or some estimate of that mean, rather than the values provided in the attached tables.

Step 2. Multiply the score for each item by the corresponding regression weight for that item and record the product in the space provided. Use the appropriate weight corresponding to the student's race and sex (white women, white men, blacks in black colleges, and blacks in white colleges).

Step 3. Sum the products and record the total in the space provided.

Step 4. Add the appropriate constant #1 to the sum and record the result in the space provided. Note the sign of the constant.

Step 5. Multiply the total by 100 and record the result. This figure equals the chances in 100 of dropping out.

Persons using these Worksheets should keep in mind several additional considerations:

First, all students who aspire to less than a bachelor's degree (for example, the associate degree) or to no degree should be omitted.

Second, any measure of actual dropout rates should carefully follow the definitions in Chapter One.

Third, no items should be omitted, and every category of categorical items (religion, race, degree plans, home town, and place of residence) should receive a score (1 or 2). If the information needed to fill in the variable score is not available, the appropriate mean should be used, except in the circumstances noted in Step 1. One other possible exception to the use of these means concerns the student's religious preference and the religion of the parents. For example, if only the student's religious preference (Religion Now) is known, it is more appropriate to assume that the parents' religion (Religion Reared) is the same than to enter the means. Similarly, if information is available only on the parents' religion, it is more appropriate to assume that the student's religion is the same. These assumptions are necessary because the weights for the regression equations were derived under circumstances where *both* parents' and students' religious preferences were known.

Somewhat more accurate estimates of dropout probabilities can be obtained by adding to the student input information data about the student's financial aid, work status, and residence during the freshman year. As shown in Chapters Three, Four, and Five, each of these classes of information adds significantly to the prediction of dropout chances. The additional steps for taking into account such data are:

Step 6. Enter information on each of the finance, work, and residence variables in the space provided.

Step 7. Multiply the variable score from Step 6 by the appropriate regression weight and record the product in the space provided.

Step 8. Sum the products obtained in Step 7 and enter the total in the space provided.

Step 9. Add the appropriate constant #2 to the total obtained in Step 8 and enter the result in the space provided.

Step 10. This is a two-stage step. First, add 1.0 to the value obtained in Step 4. Next, multiply the result by the appropriate constant #3, and enter the result in the space provided.

Step 11. Sum the results obtained in the previous two steps (9 and 10) and enter the result.

Step 12. Multiply the value from Step 11 by 100 and enter the result in the space provided. This represents the chance (in 100) of dropping out based on student-input, financial aid, work, and residence variables.

WORKSHEET—*Part One*

PREDICTING CHANCES OF DROPPING OUT USING STUDENT VARIABLES

Variable Name and Scoring	STEP 1 Enter Variable Score	REGRESSION WEIGHTS (MEAN VALUES) White Men	White Women	Blacks in Black Colleges	Blacks in White Colleges	STEP 2 Enter Product of Variable Score and Appropriate Weight
1. Average high school grade (A+ or A = 8, A— = 7, B+ = 6, B = 5, B— = 4, C+ = 3, C = 2, D = 1)	1. ‥‥‥‥‥	−.04725 (4.2839)	−.03737 (5.2047)	−.04122 (4.1426)	−.02719 (3.9739)	1. ‥‥‥‥‥
2. Rank in high school class (top 1 percent = 6, top 10 percent = 5, top quarter = 4, second quarter = 3, third quarter = 2, fourth quarter = 1)	2. ‥‥‥‥‥	−.02978 (3.4567)	−.01205 (3.9201)	−.02080 (3.7548)	−.06213 (3.3647)	2. ‥‥‥‥‥
3. College admissions test scores (combined score for SAT verbal plus mathematical)	3. ‥‥‥‥‥	−.00014 (984)	−.00029 (1002)	−.00006 (737)	−.00007 (920)	3. ‥‥‥‥‥
4. Student's academic rating of high school (very high = 5, fairly high = 4, about average = 3, probably below average = 2, definitely below average = 1)	4. ‥‥‥‥‥	−.00864 (3.9474)	−.01474 (4.0185)	−.02937 (3.6809)	−.02170 (3.8067)	4. ‥‥‥‥‥
Family Background						
5. Religion reared—Protestant (yes = 2, no = 1)	5. ‥‥‥‥‥	−.05389 (1.5130)	−.01620 (1.5418)	−.12747 (1.5555)	−.14035 (1.5434)	5. ‥‥‥‥‥
6. Religion reared—Catholic (yes = 2, no = 1)	6. ‥‥‥‥‥	−.12124 (1.3337)	.00000 (1.3222)	−.36613 (1.0431)	−.29750 (1.1533)	6. ‥‥‥‥‥

No.	Variable					No.
7.	Religion reared — Jewish (yes = 2, no = 1)	—.10309 (1.0590)	—.05026 (1.0627)	.00000 (1.0000)	—.44208 (1.0044)	7. ————
8.	Religion reared—other (yes = 2, no = 1)	—.05328 (1.0606)	—.09660 (1.0443)	—.14687 (1.3500)	—.17347 (1.2479)	8. ————
9.	Religion reared—none (yes = 2, no = 1)	—.13312 (1.0251)	.02576 (1.0222)	—.31821 (1.0154)	—.02796 (1.0114)	9. ————
10.	Religion now—Protestant (yes = 2, no = 1)	—.03078 (1.4435)	—.02740 (1.4817)	—.02371 (1.4928)	—.11759 (1.4792)	10. ————
11.	Religion now—Catholic (yes = 2, no = 1)	.00000 (1.3031)	—.07643 (1.3033)	.13241 (1.0666)	—.06529 (1.1505)	11. ————
12.	Religion now—Jewish (yes = 2, no = 1)	—.11986 (1.0511)	—.08210 (1.0549)	—.43754 (1.0010)	—.20840 (1.0019)	12. ————
13.	Religion now—other (yes = 2, no = 1)	.05581 (1.0696)	.07450 (1.0567)	—.00353 (1.3191)	—.08518 (1.2202)	13. ————
14.	Religion now—none (yes = 2, no = 1)	.07464 (1.1082)	.08703 (1.0762)	.04624 (1.0388)	—.03243 (1.0705)	14. ————
15.	Father's education (grammar school or less = 1, some high school = 2, high school graduate = 3, some college = 4, college graduate = 5, postgraduate degree = 6)	—.01691 (3.4280)	—.01066 (3.6487)	—.02431 (2.4645)	.00326 (2.7228)	15. ————
16.	Mother's education (grammar school or less = 1, some high school = 2, high school graduate = 3, some college = 4, college graduate = 5, postgraduate degree = 6)	—.01005 (3.2933)	—.01580 (3.4829)	.00237 (2.7584)	—.03910 (2.9643)	16. ————
17.	Student's concern about finances (no concern = 1, some concern = 2, major concern = 3)	.00405 (1.7418)	.03917 (1.7353)	.05743 (2.0395)	—.01690 (1.9660)	17. ————

187

WORKSHEET—*Part One* (*Continued*)

PREDICTING CHANCES OF DROPPING OUT USING STUDENT VARIABLES

Variable Name and Scoring	STEP 1 Enter Variable Score	REGRESSION WEIGHTS (MEAN VALUES) White Men	White Women	Blacks in Black Colleges	Blacks in White Colleges	STEP 2 Enter Product of Variable Score and Appropriate Weight
18. Race—Oriental (yes = 2, no = 1)	18. _____	−.07395 (1.0112)	−.09539 (1.0101)	−.08553 (1.0009)	−.10127 (1.0322)	18. _____
19. Race—other (yes = 2, no = 1)	19. _____	.03314 (1.0114)	.09119 (1.0075)	−.04165 (1.0016)	−.03786 (1.0404)	19. _____
20. Lived on a farm most of time growing up (yes = 2, no = 1)	20. _____	.04963 (1.0881)	−.04256 (1.0892)	.01104 (1.1246)	−.04669 (1.0393)	20. _____
21. Lived in a small town most of time growing up (yes = 2, no = 1)	21. _____	.05581 (1.1863)	−.01255 (1.1963)	.05125 (1.2373)	.06180 (1.1518)	21. _____
22. Lived in a moderate size city or town most of time growing up (yes = 2, no = 1)	22. _____	.01292 (1.3202)	−.01497 (1.3291)	−.00306 (1.3522)	.00517 (1.2853)	22. _____
Educational Aspirations						
23. Highest degree planned—bachelor's (yes = 2, no = 1)	23. _____	.11867 (1.3693)	.03666 (1.5135)	.05649 (1.3324)	.14308 (1.3892)	23. _____
24. Highest degree planned—master's (yes = 2, no = 1)	24. _____	.04466 (1.3422)	−.02476 (1.3662)	−.01410 (1.4016)	.01272 (1.3288)	24. _____
25. Highest degree planned—Ph.D. or Ed.D. (yes = 2, no = 1)	25. _____	.00134 (1.1653)	.00525 (1.0640)	.01827 (1.1922)	.00000 (1.1703)	25. _____

26. ———	.08016 (1.0525)	.00000 (1.0498)	.00000 (1.0234)	.00000 (1.0943)	26.
27. ———	.32027 (1.0593)	.13189 (1.0240)	.25788 (1.0329)	.23581 (1.0289)	27.
28. ———	.19658 (1.0607)	−.07980 (1.0259)	.20798 (1.0029)	.06081 (1.1603)	28.
29. ———	−.03638 (3.4097)	−.06281 (3.4740)	−.02522 (3.6149)	−.03029 (3.4194)	29.
30. ———	−.00592 (2.0881)	−.00282 (2.0193)	−.00759 (2.4311)	−.02189 (2.2512)	30.
31. ———	−.01366 (2.0067)	−.02100 (2.0254)	−.04688 (1.9143)	−.01530 (1.9948)	31.
32. ———	.04986 (3.0728)	−.00892 (3.0963)	.00943 (2.8983)	.01468 (2.8262)	32.
33. ———	.01971 (2.1280)	.03601 (2.1679)	.02843 (2.0146)	.01195 (1.8316)	33.
34. ———	.03954 (2.6639)	.02875 (2.6603)	.00555 (2.5781)	.01686 (2.5305)	34.
35. ———	.05861 (1.6285)	.00246 (1.5772)	.02822 (1.6429)	.00899 (1.8097)	35.

26. Highest degree planned—professional (yes = 2, no = 1)

27. Highest degree planned—other (yes = 2, no = 1)

28. Expects to be an engineer (yes = 2, no = 1)

Study Habits During Past Year

29. Turned in assigned work on time (always = 4, usually = 3, sometimes = 2, rarely or never = 1)

30. Did homework at the same time every day (always = 4, usually = 3, sometimes = 2, rarely or never = 1)

31. Made careless mistakes on a test (always = 4, usually = 3, sometimes = 2, rarely or never = 1)

32. Kept desk or study place neat (always = 4, usually = 3, sometimes = 2, rarely or never = 1)

33. Did extra-credit work (always = 4, usually = 3, sometimes = 2, rarely or never = 1)

34. Carefully went over diagrams or tables in textbook (always = 4, usually = 3, sometimes = 2, rarely or never = 1)

35. Was too bored to study (always = 4, usually = 3, sometimes = 2, rarely or never = 1)

WORKSHEET—*Part One* (*Continued*)

PREDICTING CHANCES OF DROPPING OUT USING STUDENT VARIABLES

Variable Name and Scoring	STEP 1 Enter Variable Score	REGRESSION WEIGHTS (MEAN VALUES)				STEP 2 Enter Product of Variable Score and Appropriate Weight
		White Men	White Women	Blacks in Black Colleges	Blacks in White Colleges	
36. Had trouble concentrating on assignments (always = 4, usually = 3, sometimes = 2, rarely or never = 1)	36. ⸺	.02058 (1.9507)	−.00619 (1.8161)	.02073 (1.9156)	.06181 (1.9192)	36. ⸺
37. Studied with radio or record player on (always = 4, usually = 3, sometimes = 2, rarely or never = 1)	37. ⸺	.01351 (1.8214)	.01715 (1.7597)	.05995 (1.8294)	−.03651 (1.8133)	37. ⸺
38. Studied alone (always = 4, usually = 3, sometimes = 2, rarely or never = 1)	38. ⸺	.00024 (3.3935)	.00000 (3.4013)	−.05626 (3.1761)	.01639 (3.3277)	38. ⸺
39. Failed to complete a homework assignment on time (frequently = 3, occasionally = 2, not at all = 1)	39. ⸺	.03399 (1.7355)	.02664 (1.5261)	.00646 (1.6625)	−.04900 (1.6722)	39. ⸺
Expectations About College ("What is your best guess as to the chances that you will . . .")						
40. Drop out temporarily (no chance = 1, very little chance = 2, some chance = 3, very good chance = 4)	40. ⸺	.04462 (1.6260)	.00303 (1.6345)	−.00776 (1.6396)	.03699 (1.5736)	40. ⸺

#	Variable		Col 1	Col 2	Col 3	Col 4	
41.	Transfer before graduating (no chance = 1, very little chance = 2, some chance = 3, very good chance = 4)	41. _____	−.01596 (2.3197)	−.00540 (2.3496)	−.04557 (2.0102)	−.05061 (2.1198)	41. _____
42.	Get married while in college (no chance = 1, very little chance = 2, some chance = 3, very good chance = 4)	42. _____	.02052 (2.0252)	.04281 (2.1971)	.00264 (1.9363)	.01264 (1.8741)	42. _____
43.	Obtain overall GPA of A− or better (no chance = 1, very little chance = 2, some chance = 3, very good chance = 4)	43. _____	.03869 (2.2579)	.04190 (2.1956)	.00279 (2.3407)	.02546 (2.3717)	43. _____
44.	Graduate with honors (no chance = 1, very little chance = 2, some chance = 3, very good chance = 4)	44. _____	.02306 (2.4842)	−.00069 (2.3768)	.01788 (2.6146)	.02490 (2.5527)	44. _____
45.	Be elected to an academic honor society (no chance = 1, very little chance = 2, some chance = 3, very good chance = 4)	45. _____	−.02961 (2.1236)	−.02492 (2.2183)	.02462 (2.3158)	−.05742 (2.1204)	45. _____

Other Student Characteristics

#	Variable		Col 1	Col 2	Col 3	Col 4	
46.	Sex (male = 1, female = 2)	46. _____	.00000 (1.0000)	.00000 (2.0000)	−.01973 (1.5739)	.00237 (1.4985)	46. _____
47.	Age at college entry (16 or younger = 1, 17 = 2, 18 = 3, 19 = 4, 20 = 5, 21 = 6, older than 21 = 7)	47. _____	.00357 (3.3403)	.03867 (3.1341)	−.01379 (3.3206)	.03457 (3.5868)	47. _____
48.	Smoked cigarettes in high school (frequently = 3, occasionally = 2, not at all = 1)	48. _____	.02550 (1.5937)	.03566 (1.4551)	.11826 (1.4484)	.10546 (1.4279)	48. _____

191

WORKSHEET—*Part One* (*Continued*)

PREDICTING CHANCES OF DROPPING OUT USING STUDENT VARIABLES

Variable Name and Scoring	STEP 1 Enter Variable Score	REGRESSION WEIGHTS (MEAN VALUES) White Men	White Women	Blacks in Black Colleges	Blacks in White Colleges	STEP 2 Enter Product of Variable Score and Appropriate Weight
49. Won varsity letter in high school (yes = 2, no = 1)	49. _____	−.05242 (1.4533)	−.02740 (1.1450)	.00463 (1.2403)	−.03967 (1.2952)	49. _____
50. Married when entering college (no = 1, yes = 2)	50. _____	−.08417 (1.0178)	.10658 (1.0198)	.02116 (1.0191)	.07893 (1.0612)	50. _____
51. Overslept and missed a class or appointment in high school (frequently = 3, occasionally = 2, not at all = 1)	51. _____	−.01238 (1.2407)	.00734 (1.1552)	.00447 (1.2116)	.03253 (1.2412)	51. _____
52. Estimate chance of marrying within year after college (no chance = 1, very little chance = 2, some chance = 3, very good chance = 4)	52. _____	−.00759 (2.5669)	−.00998 (2.7353)	−.00228 (2.3630)	.02424 (2.3292)	52. _____
CONSTANT #1:		.51853	.34803	2.03694	1.56640	

STEP 3: Sum the products obtained in Step 2 _____

STEP 4: Add the appropriate Constant #1 _____

STEP 5: Multiply by 100 _____ = chances in 100 of dropping out

Note: An approximate adjustment for errors in measurement of characteristics of entering students (see Astin, 1975) can be made by multiplying the final result from Step 5 by 1.11 and subtracting a constant from the result. The constants for the four groups are: white men, 3.4; white women, 3.0; blacks in black colleges, 2.9; blacks in white colleges, 5.6.

WORKSHEET—*Part Two*

PREDICTING CHANCES OF DROPPING OUT USING ADDITIONAL VARIABLES ON FINANCIAL AID, WORK STATUS, AND PLACE OF RESIDENCE

Variable Name and Scoring	STEP 6 Enter Variable Score	REGRESSION WEIGHTS				STEP 7 Enter Product of Variable Score and Appropriate Weight
		White Men	White Women	Blacks in Black Colleges	Blacks in White Colleges	
Sources of Financial Aid During Freshman Year						
53. Personal savings and/or employment (major support = 3, minor support = 2, not a source = 1)	53. _____	.00189 (2.102)	.00443 (1.804)	−.00225 (1.510)	−.02215 (1.761)	53. _____
54. Parental or other family aid (major support = 3, minor support = 2, not a source = 1)	54. _____	−.01243 (2.194)	−.02534 (2.485)	−.00548 (1.920)	−.03446 (1.905)	54. _____
55. Repayable loan (major support = 3, minor support = 2, not a source = 1)	55. _____	.03052 (1.340)	−.00553 (1.399)	.00474 (1.792)	−.04614 (1.493)	55. _____
56. Scholarship, grant, or other gift (major support = 3, minor support = 2, not a source = 1)	56. _____	−.02177 (1.470)	−.01130 (1.533)	−.01819 (1.786)	−.03308 (1.809)	56. _____
Work Status During Freshman Year						
57. Federally sponsored work-study program (yes = 2, no = 1)	57. _____	−.02007 (1.024)	−.04994 (1.052)	−.15420 (1.111)	−.09535 (1.119)	57. _____
58. Other on-campus work (yes = 2, no = 1)	58. _____	−.03132 (1.063)	−.03949 (1.086)	−.00036 (1.044)	−.12293 (1.059)	58. _____
59. Off-campus work (yes = 2, no = 1)	59. _____	−.07779 (1.219)	−.04612 (1.151)	.04234 (1.075)	−.07201 (1.138)	59. _____
60. Employment for college credit as part of departmental program (yes = 2, no = 1)	60. _____	−.04905 (1.021)	.03811 (1.004)	.39389 (1.002)	−.11783 (1.007)	60. _____

193

WORKSHEET—Part Two (Continued)

PREDICTING CHANCES OF DROPPING OUT USING ADDITIONAL VARIABLES ON FINANCIAL AID, WORK STATUS, AND PLACE OF RESIDENCE

Variable Name and Scoring	STEP 6 Enter Variable Score	REGRESSION WEIGHTS				STEP 7 Enter Product of Variable Score and Appropriate Weight
		White Men	White Women	Blacks in Black Colleges	Blacks in White Colleges	
61. Number of hours worked per week (25 or more = 6, 20–24 = 5, 15–19 = 4, 10–14 = 3, 5–9 = 2, fewer than 5 = 1)	61. ———	.01898 (3.425)	.01069 (2.830)	−.01641 (2.941)	.01772 (3.629)	61. ———
Place of Residence During Freshman Year						
62. College dormitory (yes = 2, no = 1)	62. ———	−.12709 (1.505)	−.12237 (1.642)	−.13246 (1.686)	−.06512 (1.428)	62. ———
63. With parents (yes = 2, no = 1)	63. ———	.00865 (1.382)	−.01113 (1.302)	.02303 (1.247)	.03238 (1.443)	63. ———
64. Other (yes = 2, no = 1)	64. ———	.00000 (1.114)	.00000 (1.067)	.00000 (1.067)	.00000 (1.129)	64. ———
CONSTANT #2		−.74759	−.57726	−.98557	−.17663	
CONSTANT #3		1.05478	.96388	.99844	.88590	

STEP 8: Sum the products obtained in Step 7 ———

STEP 9: Add the appropriate Constant #2 ———

STEP 10: Add 1.0 to the value from Step 4, multiply the result by appropriate Constant #3, and enter product ———

STEP 11: Sum the results from Steps 9 and 10 ———

STEP 12: Multiply by 100 ——— = chances in 100 of dropping out

REFERENCES

ALFERT, E. "Housing Selection, Need Satisfaction, and Dropout from College." *Psychological Reports*, 1966, *19*, 183–186.

ASTIN, A. W. "An Empirical Characterization of Higher Educational Institutions." *Journal of Educational Psychology*, 1962, *53*, 224–235.

ASTIN, A. W. "Personal and Environmental Factors Associated with College Dropouts Among High Aptitude Students." *Journal of Educational Psychology*, 1964, *55*, 276–287.

ASTIN, A. W. *Who Goes Where To College?* Chicago: Science Research Associates, 1965.

ASTIN, A. W. *The College Environment*. Washington, D.C.: American Council on Education, 1968.

ASTIN, A. W. "How Colleges Are Rated." *Change* Magazine, November/December, 1970.

ASTIN, A. W. *Predicting Academic Performance in College*. New York: Free Press, 1971.

ASTIN, A. W. *College Dropouts: A National Profile*. ACE Research Reports. Washington, D.C.: American Council on Education, 1972a.

ASTIN, A. W. "The Measured Effects of Higher Education." The *Annals* of The American Academy of Political and Social Science, 1972b, *404*, 1–20.

ASTIN, A. W. "Impact of Dormitory Living on Students." *Educational Record*, 1973, *54* (3).

ASTIN, A. W. *Dropouts, Stopouts, and Persisters: A National Profile*. Los

Angeles: Laboratory for Research on Higher Education, University of California, 1975.

ASTIN, A. W., and CHRISTIAN, C. E. *The Allocation of Financial Aid by Sex, Race, and Parental Income Level.* Unpublished manuscript. Los Angeles: Higher Education Research Institute, 1975.

ASTIN, A. W., KING, M. R., LIGHT, J. M., and RICHARDSON, G. T. *The American Freshman: National Norms for Fall 1974.* Los Angeles: Graduate School of Education, University of California, 1974.

ASTIN, A. W., and LEE, C. B. T. *The Invisible Colleges.* New York: McGraw-Hill, 1971.

ASTIN, A. W., and MOLM, L. D. *Correcting for Nonresponse Bias in Follow-up Surveys.* Unpublished manuscript. Washington, D.C.: American Council on Education, 1972.

ASTIN, A. W., and PANOS, R. J. *The Educational and Vocational Development of College Students.* Washington, D.C.: American Council on Education, 1969.

ASTIN, H. S. *Educational Progress of Disadvantaged Students.* Washington, D.C.: Bureau of Social Science Research, Inc., 1970.

BABER, B. B., JR., and CAPLE, R. B. "Educational Opportunity Grant Students: Persisters and Nonpersisters." *The Journal of College Student Personnel,* 1970, *11,* 115–119.

BAYER, A. E. "The College Dropout: Factors Affecting Senior College Completion." *Sociology of Education,* 1968, *41,* 305–316.

BAYER, A. E. "Marriage Plans and Educational Aspirations." *American Journal of Sociology,* September 1969, 239–244.

BAYER, A. E., and BORUCH, R. F. "Black and White Freshmen Entering Four-Year Colleges." *Educational Record,* Winter 1969.

BAYER, A. E., ROYER, J. T., and WEBB, R. M. *Four Years After College Entry.* ACE Research Reports. Washington, D.C.: American Council on Education, 1973.

BLANCHFIELD, W. C. "College Dropout Identification: A Case Study." *The Journal of Experimental Education,* 1971, *40,* 1–4.

BRAWER, F. B. *New Perspectives on Personality Development in College Students.* San Francisco: Jossey-Bass, 1973.

Carnegie Commission on Higher Education. *More Time, Less Options.* New York: McGraw-Hill, 1972.

CHASE, C. I. "The College Dropout: His High School Prologue." *Bulletin* of the National Association of Secondary School Principals, 1970, *54,* 67–71.

CHICKERING, A. W. *Commuters Versus Residents*. San Francisco: Jossey-Bass, 1974.

COHEN, A. M., BRAWER, F. B., and CONNOR, A. *Selected Personality Correlates of Junior College Dropouts and Persisters*. Paper read at California Educational Research Association. Los Angeles, March, 1969.

COPE, R. G. "Types of High Ability Dropouts Who Continue in College." *The North Central Association Quarterly*, 1969, *44*, 253–256.

COPE, R. G. "Sex-Related Factors and Attrition Among College Women." *Journal of the National Association of Women Deans and Counselors*, 1970, *31*, 118–124.

COPE, R. G. "Are Students More Likely to Drop Out of Large Colleges?" *College Student Journal*, 1972, *6*, 92–97.

DE VECCHIO, R. C. "Characteristics of Nonreturning Community College Freshmen." *The Journal of College Student Personnel*, 1972, *13*, 429–432.

DI CESARE, A. C., SEDLACEK, W. E., and BROOKS, G. C., JR. "Nonintellectual Correlates of Black Student Attrition." *The Journal of College Student Personnel*, 1972, *13*, 319–324.

DVORAK, E. J. "Educational and Personality Characteristics of Smokers and Nonsmokers Among University Freshmen." *The Journal of the American College Health Association*, 1967, *16*, 80–84.

EAGLE, N. *Dropout Prediction at an Urban Community College Following Open Admissions*. Paper read at American Educational Research Association meeting. New Orleans, February, 1973.

HANNAH, W. "Personality Differentials Between Lower Division Dropouts and Stay-ins." *The Journal of College Student Personnel*, 1971, *12*, 16–19.

HILL, A. H. "A Longitudinal Study of Attrition Among High Aptitude College Students." *The Journal of Educational Research*, 1966, *60*, 166–173.

JOHNSON, D. E. "Personality Characteristics in Relation to College Persistence." *Journal of Counseling Psychology*, 1970, *17*, 162–167.

KOSHER, E. W., and BELLAMY, R. Q. "Some Background Differences Between College Graduates and Dropouts." *Psychology*, 1969, *6*, 1–6.

KRAMER, L. A., and KRAMER, M. B. "The College Library and the Drop-Out." *College and Research Libraries*, 1968, *29*, 310–312.

LINDQUIST, E. F. "An Evaluation of a Technique for Scaling High

School Grades to Improve Prediction of College Grades." *Educational and Psychological Measurement*, 1963, *23*, 623–646.

MACK, F. R.-P. "Predicting College Persistence for Educational Opportunity Students." *Psychology*, 1973, *10*, 14-28.

MAC MILLAN, T. F. "NORCAL: The Key Is Cooperation." *Junior College Journal*, 1970, *40*, 28–31.

Middle States Accrediting Association. Evaluating Team Report for Empire State College, November 1974.

MILLER, A. J., and TWYMAN, J. P. "Persistence in Engineering and Technical Institute Programs: A Study of Some Nonintellective Concomitants." *The Journal of Human Resources*, 1967, *2*, 254–262.

MORRISEY, R. J. "Attrition in Probationary Freshmen." *The Journal of College Student Personnel*, 1971, *12*, 279–285.

NELSON, A. G. "College Characteristics Associated with Freshman Attrition." *The Personnel and Guidance Journal*, 1966, *44*, 1046–1050.

NEWMAN, M. A. *The Student and the College Community: A Study of Attrition and Persistence in a Highly Selective Liberal Arts College.* Cooperative Research Project No. S-130. Chicago: University of Chicago, 1965.

PACE, C. R. *The Demise of Diversity: A Comparative Profile of Eight Types of Institutions.* New York: McGraw-Hill, 1974.

PUMROY, D. K. "Cigarette Smoking and Academic Achievement." *The Journal of General Psychology*, 1967, *77*, 31–34.

SNYDER, B. " 'Creative' Students in Science and Engineering." *Universities Quarterly*, March 1967, 205–218.

SUMMERSKILL, J. "Dropouts from College." In N. Sanford (Ed.), *The American College.* New York: Wiley, 1962.

TRAPP, D., PAILTHORP, K., and COPE, R. "Entrance Characteristics and Their Relationship to Types of Student Dropouts." In *Institutional Research and Institutional Policy Formulation: 11th Annual Forum of the Association for Institutional Research 1971.* Claremont, Calif.: Office of Institutional Research, 1971.

TRENT, J. W., and MEDSKER, L. L. *Beyond High School: A Study of 10,000 High School Graduates.* Berkeley: Center for Research and Development in Higher Education, University of California, 1967.

WEGNER, E. L., and SEWELL, W. H. "Selection and Context as Factors Affecting the Probability of Graduating from College." *American Journal of Sociology*, 1967, *75*, 665–679.

INDEX

199